DERBY ROAD

BOVRIL

THE WHISKY DEWAR'S White Label

9

146

NOTTINGHAM CORPORATION TRAMWAYS

B.G.NICKHOLDS

BUSES, TROLLEYS & TRAMS

CHAS. S. DUNBAR

CONTENTS

First published in 1967 by The Hamlyn Publishing Group Ltd
This edition published 2004 by Bounty Books, a division of
Octopus Publishing Group Ltd, 2-4 Heron Quays, London E14 4JP
Copyright © 1967 Octopus Publishing Group Ltd
Reprinted 2005
ISBN 0 7537 0970 8
ISBN 13 9780753 709702

Printed and bound in China

AUTHOR'S PREFACE

In this book I have tried within limits to describe the history and development over the last century and a half of public road transport, in all its many forms.

The task of selecting material and compressing it into a book of this scope was formidable and some readers may feel that I have given insufficient attention to the aspect of transport in which they are especially interested. This is perhaps inevitable, but from my efforts I hope that the specialists will find a useful source for reference to dates and major events, and that younger readers will be encouraged to go on for themselves and find out more about transport and its history.

I could not have written this book without the previous work of Charles E. Lee who, besides allowing me to draw on his great knowledge of the subject, has been good enough to read through my manuscript; Charles F. Klapper ('The Golden Age of Tramways'); T. C. Barker and R. M. Robbins ('A History of London Transport'); E. L. Cornwell ('Commercial Road Vehicles'); J. Robert ('Les Tramways Parisiens'); F. Rowsome and S. D. Maguire ('Trolley Car Treasury'); L. A. G. Strong ('The Rolling Road'); the late F. M. Atkins; G. E. Baddeley; M. Gibson; J. C. Gillham; W. Gratwicke; S. E. Harrison; A. G. Jenson; J. Joyce; the late O. J. Morris; J. F. Parke; J. H. Price; G. J. Robbins; A. A. Townsin; J. S. Webb; W. J. Wyse and many other members of the Omnibus Society, the Light Railway Transport League, the Tramway and Light Railway Society, the Tramway Museum Society and the Transport Ticket Society.

CHAS. S. DUNBAR

QUICKER THAN WALKING

For the greater part of the period Man has been on earth, the majority of human beings have had no reason or desire to go further than their two legs could carry them. Even in the highly complex industrial civilizations of the West there are still thousands who have never gone more than a few miles from the place of their birth.

Mass movements of whole tribes began, perhaps five or six thousand years ago, because of the need to seek new sources of food supply but, in general, the individual did not stray from his fellows. As time went on, daring men began to explore other countries than their own but their movements were largely by water. It was only as settled agricultural systems developed, that any thought of regular trade entered men's heads.

Trade brought into existence a system of tracks and one such, it seems, was established in Britain before the Romans came. Many of these ancient ways formed the basis of the military roads which the invaders built to consolidate their position, but when they left, their roads gradually fell into decay.

The disrepair of the highways did not prohibit movement but it limited the use of wheeled vehicles, while the social effect of the feudal system was to rivet the great majority of people to the place of their birth. The virtual collapse of feudalism after the Black Death and the growing importance of the towns from the fifteenth century onwards gradually led to an increase in land communications.

By the reign of James I there were a great number of regular carrier services connecting all the principal centres of England and Wales with London. The wagons used on these services carried passengers but the state of the roads made this form of travel an extremely slow business. Wealthy people usually travelled on horseback, as did the post boys. The Royal Mail can trace its origins back to the fifteenth century but it was not until 1784 that it began to be conveyed by wheeled vehicles.

Before this happened, the growth of London and of other large cities abroad prompted the building of coaches for the well-to-do. These were copied and adapted for public transport on definite routes and so became stage-coaches. About the same time, from

In colour, top: A two-ton Gurney steam carriage on the Bath-London road, 1829. Bottom: A country horse-bus preserved in the Clapham Transport Museum in London
Above: The first mail-coach entered service on the Bristol-London route on August 2, 1784

1633 onward, hackney-coaches appeared in London. These were vehicles which could be found waiting for individual hire at a particular stand—the start, in fact, of the present-day taxi rank.

The philosopher Blaise Pascal started a service of *carosses à cinq sols* in Paris in 1662, but this facility of vehicles running on five regular routes and available to anyone did not last long. The government unwisely forbade the use of these coaches by the *gens du peuple* and so killed potential custom. By 1675 the service had ceased.

August 2nd, 1784 is an important date in transport history for on that day John Palmer, a Bath theatre proprietor, having secured a contract with the Post Office, started a regular service of mail-coaches between Bristol and London, which, in addition to the mails, carried passengers also. The feature of these mail-coaches which distinguished them from the stage-coaches was the armed guard, who was in government employ. They did not have to pay turnpike tolls and the arrangements for frequent changes of horses which were an essential part of the system enabled a high average speed to be maintained, particularly after the great road improvements engineered by Metcalfe, Loudon, Telford and Macadam.

But coaching was expensive and beyond the means of most persons, so that when the nineteenth century opened, most people in Britain (and in Europe generally), if they travelled at all, did so on foot. In the towns most people lived near their work or else expected naturally to walk to and from it.

It was in France that urban passenger transport on present-day lines really began. Jacques Lafitte is said to have started a regular service in Paris in 1819 but details of this are vague. What is certain is that in 1823 Stanislas Baudry, who owned some hot baths in a suburb of Nantes, began running vehicles to them from a stand in the Place du Commerce. This stand was at a shop belonging to a M. Omnes who had adopted the slogan *Omnes omnibus*, 'Omnes for all.' Baudry soon found that people were using his vehicles who did not want to go to the baths. He gave the carriages the title of omnibus and set about building up a transport business.

In 1828 he obtained powers to start 12 routes in Paris. His success produced a great number of competitors and a great demand for vehicles. Among the builders of these was an Englishman, George Shillibeer. He was struck with the lightness and consequent speed of the vehicles which were then being

made in Paris and with the business which they were attracting. He sold his coach-building business and returned to England.

The growth of London had led to the development of short stage services. The vehicles employed were heavy and slow and the fares, as for the mail and long distance stages, were expensive and beyond most people's means. Shillibeer built two 22-seat three-horse buses and on July 4th, 1829 began a regular time-tabled service with them from either Paddington Green or 'The Yorkshire Stingo' in Marylebone Road to the Bank via New Road (now Euston Road and City Road) at a fare of a shilling (compared with 1s. 6d inside and 1s. outside a stage-coach) or 6d. to and from Islington and either terminus. Nor was it necessary to go through the cumbrous process of booking before boarding a vehicle. Although picking up and setting down at intermediate points was not legal until the passing of the Stage Coach Act, 1832, Shillibeer's vehicles apparently stopped anywhere. Shillibeer's success attracted a horde of competitors and he was eventually forced out of the bus business and ended his days as an undertaker.

Until well into the twentieth century the London bus was more of a middle-class conveyance than one for the manual workers and this aspect is shown in a petition which Shillibeer sent to the government when a bill was under consideration to relieve stage coaches of mileage duty and to legalize picking-up and setting-down in the streets of the city proper. He spoke of the advantages of the omnibus, 'especially to the middling class of trades-people whose finances cannot admit of the accommodation of a hackney coach and are therefore necessitated to lose that time in walking which might be beneficially devoted to business at home.'

Parallel with these developments others were taking place which had an even greater effect on inland transport and in the long run on human progress throughout the world.

As early as the second half of the sixteenth century coal and ore from mines in the Midlands and the north of England was moving in sufficient quantities to cause thought to be given to the possibility of easing the burden on the horses who pulled the primitive wagons. It was found that a double row of timber baulks laid lengthways, end to end, and with just sufficient width between the rows to accommodate the average width between wagon wheels, helped considerably; so did stone setts laid in parallel rows. Later

these gave way to iron plates. In course of time the plates were fitted with flanges so that wagon wheels could not go off the track. The original timber baulks were called trams and from these came the word tramroad or tramway, used before long whether the way was of wood, stone or iron. (It is a common fallacy that tramway is derived from an engineer named Outram.) When the use of iron plates with flanges became common and these began to be specially made for the job, the word railway or railroad came into use.

The early tramways or railways were built to serve individual pits or quarries or, in the last quarter of the eighteenth century, to feed the growing network of canals. The Surrey Iron Railway from Wandsworth to Croydon, authorized in May, 1801, was the first to be constructed independently of a canal. There followed two others in South Wales and an extension of the Surrey line. Then, in 1804, an Act was passed to incorporate the Oystermouth Railway or Tramroad Company.

As with other early railways, the Oystermouth Company provided a public road and it was available to any vehicle whose owners were prepared to pay the stipulated tolls. The importance of the line is that

it provided the world's first public service by rail. A man named Benjamin French offered the company a payment of £20 a year in commutation of tolls for permission to run a wagon for the conveyance of passengers. The offer was accepted and French's vehicle which was, of course, horse-drawn, started work on March 25th, 1807.

Charles E. Lee in his *The Swansea and Mumbles Railway* quoted several authors who enjoyed the ride to Oystermouth and also one who did not. This was Richard Ayton who in *A Voyage round Great Britain in the year 1813* used a name for the vehicle which has since passed into common use. He said:

'We made an excursion to Oystermouth village near the western extremity of Swansea Bay, in the tram car, a singular kind of vehicle established for the accommodation of visitors to this place. It is a very long carriage, supported on four low iron wheels, carries sixteen persons, exclusive of the driver, is drawn by one horse, and rolls along over an iron rail-road, at the rate of five miles an hour, and with the noise of twenty sledge hammers in full play. The passage is only four miles, but it is quite sufficient to make one reel from the car at the journey's end, in a state of

dizziness and confusion of the senses that it is well if he recovers from in a week.'

The passenger service seems to have been withdrawn about 1827 but was resumed, again with horse traction, in 1860.

The Surrey and Oystermouth railways came into being as the influence of the Industrial Revolution was transforming Britain from a predominantly agricultural to a predominantly industrial country. Steam was the driving force of the revolution and when steam engines had proved their reliability, it was natural that men's thoughts should turn to the possibility of using this power for traction. Stationary engines could obviously be used for pulling loaded wagons up gradients too steep for horses but early attempts to build a reliable locomotive were not very successful.

George Stephenson experimented with steam engines on the colliery railway at Killingworth, near Newcastle-on-Tyne and, when the Stockton and Darlington Railway was opened in 1825, proved that steam traction on railways for goods and passengers was perfectly feasible. As a result the Liverpool and Manchester Railway was opened in 1830 to operate a steam-hauled service exclusively.

The application of steam to coaching was also

tried, but the first steam-driven road vehicles such as Trevithick's, which made demonstration runs in Cornwall in 1801 and in London in 1803, aroused little interest. In 1826, however, Sir Goldsworthy Gurney developed a boiler using a series of U-shaped water tubes with the fire built directly on the lower arms of the tubes which proved in practice to be reliable and efficient. A mixture of coke and charcoal was used for firing. Steam was delivered to a two-cylinder engine developing 12 h.p.

In 1831, Sir Charles Dance started a regular service between Gloucester and Cheltenham using a coach fitted with a Gurney boiler and engine, these being mounted over the rear axle. The vehicle itself resembled the usual horse-drawn coach except that ahead of the front axle was a forward portion with small wheels corresponding to the tractor in a modern articulated vehicle, except, of course, that it had no engine. Its sole purpose was to steer the vehicle. The driver sat fairly low down and used a tiller for this purpose. It is not clear from extant paintings where the engine and brake controls were placed but it is known that brakes operated on the rims of the rear wheels and, in an emergency, the engine could be reversed for braking. Steering was one of the weak

points of early mechanical vehicles. Ackermann patented a steering system resembling a modern layout in 1818 but no one would take it up for many years after. The coach on Dance's service seated six inside and 12 outside. It ran for four months and carried over 3,000 passengers.

Another inventor who achieved an even greater success was Walter Hancock who patented a modified water-tube boiler in 1827. From this he went on to develop boilers with forced draught provided by an engine-driven fan, a clutch which permitted fan and water pump to be operated while the vehicle was stationary, and other improvements. In 1831 he started a service between Stratford (Essex) and London with a four-wheeled ten-seat coach called 'The Infant' and later put larger vehicles to work on Shillibeer's original route. Hancock's services continued until about 1840.

Another notable steam service was that between Paisley and Glasgow operated by Scott Russell for four months in 1834. It looked as if it would continue indefinitely but after the boiler on one of the vehicles exploded and killed five people, the Court of Session stopped the service.

During the 1830s many improvements were made to steam engines and the creation of a nation-wide network of services seemed a future possibility, but there was much hostility to the new vehicles, particularly on the part of the landowners and turnpike trusts. By 1850 mechanical road transport in Britain was practically dead, except in the form of traction engines.

The great application of steam was, of course, to the railways, which expanded with tremendous rapidity and in a relatively short time had, with few exceptions, driven mail-coaches, stage-coaches and stage-wagons off the roads. Only purely local traffic was left for road transport and the road system itself deteriorated as a result.

As the Industrial Revolution advanced, improved means of communication within the sprawling towns, swollen by the influx of workers, became increasingly necessary. We have seen how Shillibeer led the way in London and how an early changeover from horse traction to steam did not take place as might have been expected. There was, however, another development of far-reaching consequence. London had fairly well-paved main streets in 1830. Many fast-growing American towns had anything but well-paved streets and the earliest omnibuses, starting some time

in the 1820s (exact records seem to be very scarce), were far from comfortable to ride in. Rail transport offered a smoother journey and it is not surprising, therefore, that street railways appeared much earlier in America than in Britain.

(At this point it should be mentioned that what, broadly speaking, to a Briton is a tramway with tramcars is to an American a street railway with streetcars. When electrification came, Americans began to speak of trolleycars or later, trolleys, but this term has never been used in Britain. Trolleybuses have sometimes been called trolleys for short.)

There is a record of a street railway in Baltimore as early as 1828 and there may have been other experiments, but the best authenticated of the early lines started in Manhattan in 1832, oddly enough as a 'downtown' prolongation of a proposed steam railway.

A young Irishman, John Stephenson, who had set up in New York as a coachbuilder, foresaw the advantage of rail communication up the Hudson Valley and secured the interest of other businessmen to form a company for a New York and Harlaem (as it was originally spelt) railroad. Although the State Legislature authorized the double-track line, New York's city fathers were hostile to the idea of steam locomo-

tives running in the streets. They agreed to horse traction and Stephenson, therefore, designed a vehicle strongly resembling the usual stage-coach of the period. It had three upholstered compartments, each entered either side from the running boards. There were seats for 30 inside and it is said that 30 more could be accommodated on the roof. A drawing of Stephenson's first vehicle (called 'John Mason' after the president of the company) shows what might have been a sort of bench along the roof similar to the later 'knifeboard', but, if this were used, the seat must have been a precarious one.

SIDE VIEW OF THE OMNIBUS.

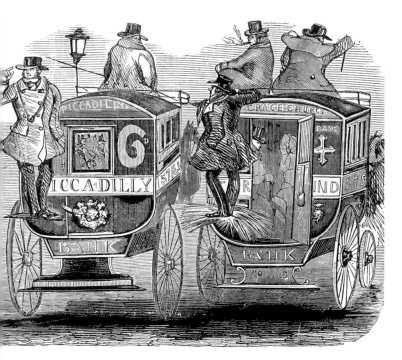

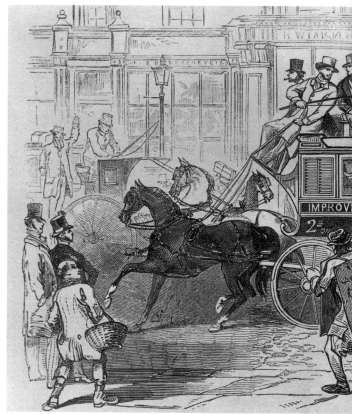

Although the new line worked well it was not until 1837 that it actually reached Harlem. Despite the original prohibition, steam locomotives were used from time to time but from 1845 the line was continuously operated by horses. Other American cities were slow to follow New York's example (except that New Orleans had a four-mile line in 1835) but from 1851 onwards the 'animal railway' became a familiar part of the scene in the larger towns. In Boston, one of the few cities where street cars still run, the Cambridge Railroad was opened on March 26th, 1856.

Stephenson's stage-coach design was soon abandoned for one more resembling the omnibuses of the time—single-deck vehicles with the driver sitting on the roof in front and passengers getting in by steps leading to a door in the centre of the back. Fare collection was not easy when these vehicles were one-man operated, as money had to be passed up to the driver through a flap in the roof. This before long made conductors a necessity on busy routes.

There was also the problem of turning the cars at the end of a journey. Sometimes turntables were laid down where the tracks ended, but to avoid this expense and to enable cars to be turned anywhere, several designs were evolved which enabled the whole body to be swung round while the underframe remained stationary. It was not until somewhere about 1860 that double-ended cars with platforms came into use. The bus influence in tramcar design lasted long after this date. Because of the bad road surfaces early buses had large wheels and these made it necessary to sweep the body out over them to give adequate seating. Although cars on street railways did not need large wheels, this shape of body persisted in a modified form right into the days of electric working. The rocker panel, as the lower part of the body side was called, was clearly seen on nearly all British buses

Why not go a step further, as above?

until as late as 1919, and was then abandoned.

In Europe during the period 1830 to 1850 urban transport development was, generally speaking, by horse drawn bus. The services in Paris, referred to earlier, expanded rapidly. The fierce competition led to many bankruptcies and later to a scheme of consolidation which had far-reaching results.

In London the problem of unregulated competition was tackled at an early date. On September 10th, 1831, the operators on the Paddington-Bank route formed an association with Shillibeer as first chairman. Of the 90 buses on the road, 33 were withdrawn and the others were organized to give a three-minute service throughout the day from 8 a.m. to 10 p.m. Inspectors, appointed by the association, were stationed at strategic points on the route to enforce proper timekeeping. As other services were opened up in the London area, similar associations came into being usually after a brief period of uneconomic competition. In their most developed form the associations employed the conductors and inspectors as well as allocating 'times' to the individual members who supplied the horses, vehicles and drivers.

Shillibeer's first bus with three horses proved too heavy and cumbersome for central city streets and lighter two-horse vehicles seating only 12 to 15 became general. At some time in the early 1840s one or two passengers were allowed to sit beside the driver on the roof. Then some vehicles were adapted to take a second row behind the driver. Buses began to be built with curved roofs and by the middle of the decade agile male passengers were clambering up and sitting on these in the peak periods. Then in April, 1847, came the clerestory roof, first shown in buses built by Adams of Bow. These were definitely designed to encourage outside passengers who were given the inducement of lower fares.

THE HORSE SUPREME

The Great Exhibition of 1851 probably did more than any other single event of the nineteenth century to foster the urge to see places other than one's own locality. Special trains from the provinces brought thousands into London and the bus proprietors reaped a rich harvest. Many, who had hesitated to carry outside passengers, hastened to provide rough accommodation on the roofs of their vehicles by fixing a board the length of the roof on which people could sit back to back. Some wag soon named this 'the knifeboard', having in mind the board covered with rough emery paper on which cutlery was cleaned until the invention of stainless steel.

The clerestory roof, already referred to, gave more comfortable seating for outside passengers and a large vehicle of this type, seating 42 all told, and drawn by three horses, was put on the road in Manchester in 1852. Double-deckers were also, apparently, coming into use in Belgium; the writer of a letter to *The Times* in 1851 said that buses there were fitted with a spiral staircase instead of the rungs by which English passengers had to mount to the top.

By this time buses were commonplace in all large towns in Europe. Hamburg had a service from 1839, Copenhagen from 1841 and Berlin from 1846.

It is not known if the fierce competition in Paris in the 1830s and '40s produced anything comparable to the London associations but, by 1855, there were only ten undertakings at work. They had a total of about 300 vehicles. The energetic Baron Haussman, who did so much to improve traffic flow in the French capital during the Second Empire, brought about the fusion of these ten companies by imperial decree dated February 22nd, 1855. The new organization was at first called L'Entreprise Générale des Omnibus, but soon became La Compagnie Générale des Omnibus. It was given a monopoly inside the fortifications of Paris. The fleet was raised to 500 vehicles and all the new buses were fitted with outside seating (*l'impériale*).

About this time conditions in London were distinctly uncomfortable for the bus proprietors. So great had been the demand for transport in 1851 that many newcomers had got in on the associations' routes. When the Exhibition closed there was an excess of capacity on the streets and fares were drastically cut. This state of affairs came to the notice of Joseph Orsi, a French financier and close friend of Napoleon III, who had an office in London and who was also one of the promoters of the C.G.O. in Paris. He and another business man, Léopold Foucaud, decided to

sound the London bus proprietors on the subject of amalgamation.

They did not meet with immediate success but, nevertheless, formed in Paris in December, 1855, La Compagnie Générale des Omnibus de Londres. In the following month the new company began taking over existing businesses and in a little over a year had close on 600 buses in its fleet, so becoming easily the largest street transport undertaking in the world at that time. Some prominent proprietors refused to sell out and two of them, Thomas Tilling and the Birch family continued to provide services in the metropolis for many years after. Tilling, in fact, operated London services without a break until 1933. Thus the new company did not obtain complete control of the associations, which continued to exist to the end of the horse-traction era.

Control from Paris proved unsatisfactory and from January 1st, 1859, the business was transferred to a British-registered London General Omnibus Co. Ltd. From then onwards French participation declined.

One of the first moves of the new company had been to produce a better type of bus. An open competition did not produce a single wholly satisfactory design but a standard type with 'knifeboard' seating on the upper deck was evolved and produced.

The year 1855 has another claim to fame, an event much less known than the formation of the two great companies in London and Paris, but one which had far-reaching effects. This was the opening of the first permanent street railway in Europe. The development of this form of conveyance greatly affected the growth of urban communities in all the industrialized countries and particularly in Britain.

It was in Paris that the new form of transport first established itself in Europe. Alphonse Loubat, who had had experience with street railways in America, asked for powers for a line from Vincennes to Sèvres and to Boulogne, but was told to give a demonstration first. This he did in November, 1853 on a line along the Quai de Billy (now the Quai de New York) and the Quai de la Conférence.

Although as a result Loubat was given a concession, he was prohibited from operating east of the Place de la Concorde. His service, the Chemin de Fer Américain, as it was called, started in September, 1855. The following year Loubat sold out to the Compagnie Générale des Omnibus. In 1866 there was a curious development. The line was extended to the Louvre but as a bus service. At Cours la Reine the flanged

wheels of the cars were taken off and flangeless ones substituted; at the same time a third horse was attached as the two which could pull a 40-seat car on rails could not do so over the roads. This time-wasting arrangement lasted until June, 1873 when the tram tracks were at last extended to the Louvre.

Paris thus led the way but it was not until the 1870s that trams really began to play an important part in the city's transport system, although a line from Sèvres to Versailles was opened as early as 1857.

Loubat's idea struck the imagination of William Joseph Curtis, an Englishman who had had tramway experience in America and who as early as 1838 had patented a system of cable traction. He designed a mechanism for changing flanged to flangeless wheels and vice versa and in March, 1859 was able, with the consent of the dock authorities, to start a service of 'railway omnibuses' on the tracks which carried goods trains along the line of docks in Liverpool. Unfortunately for Curtis the Mersey Docks and Harbour Board allowed several local bus proprietors who were already in business to put similar vehicles to work. They were popular with the public but so disorganized the working of goods trains that, after only nine months' operation, the experiment came to an end and Liverpool

Right: The first horse car at the Cape, South Africa, seen here with an impressive load of local dignitaries

Centre: Casebolt's balloon car in San Francisco, built to swivel round

Below: A car on G. F. Train's Victoria Street line in London

continued until 1869 to rely for street transport on the horse buses which had served it since the 1830s.

It was on the other side of the Mersey in Birkenhead that the first tramway was laid in England which was to have a continuous existence until it was superseded by motor buses. This was due to the activities of George Francis Train, a flamboyant young American only just turned 30, whose family had long been connected with shipping and thus had contacts with Merseyside. He obtained permission from Birkenhead Town Commissioners to lay tracks from Woodside Ferry to Birkenhead Park and service started on this route on August 30th, 1860. Unfortunately, Train built his line with L-shaped step-rails, laid with the vertical portion projecting ¾ in. above the sole of the rail and so above the level of the roadway. Not surprisingly, he was soon in trouble with the local carriage and wagon owners, so that before long the track had to be relaid with grooved rails.

One would have thought that after this experience Train would have realized that the step rail had no chance of permanent adoption but he persuaded the Local Board in West Derby (then outside Liverpool) to agree to a line from the Liverpool boundary to Old Swan which he laid with step rails and opened in

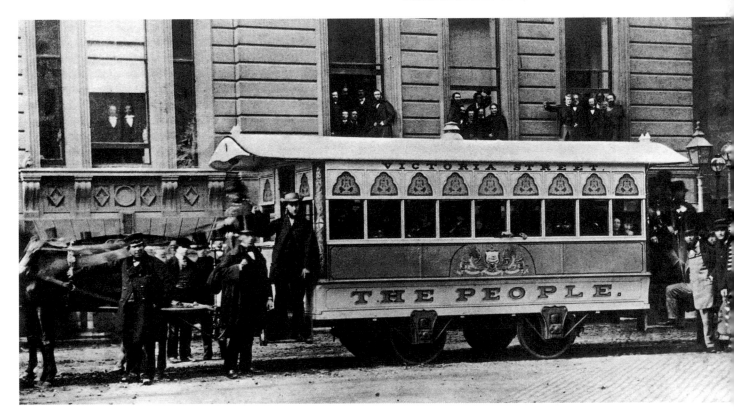

July, 1861. This enjoyed only a very short life.

Meantime Train had turned his attention to London. He was not the first to think of introducing trams to the capital. Not surprisingly in view of its Parisian connections, the London General, while still under French control, considered the possibility of doing so and went so far as to form the London Omnibus Tramway Co. Ltd. and to promote a double-track line from Notting Hill Gate to the Bank, with a branch from King's Cross to Fleet Street. Unfortunately the then Chief Commissioner of Public Works, Sir Benjamin Hall (whose name is commemorated in 'Big Ben') was determined, if he could, to stop rails being laid in the London streets. His hostility is said to have resulted from his carriage having been overturned when crossing plateways in South Wales. The fact that the General's subsidiary proposed to use rails flush with the street surface did not mitigate his opposition.

Having failed themselves, the managers of the General did not let Train get in without a fight, but eventually he was allowed to lay three demonstration lines—in Bayswater Road (opened March 23rd, 1861), Victoria Street (April 15th, 1861) and Kennington Road (August 15th, 1861). All three lines had a very

short life, mainly because of the hostility the step rail aroused. The Westminster Bridge - Kennington Gate line gave promise of being a great success and did, in later years, carry some of the heaviest tramway traffic in London, but no trams ever subsequently ran in either Bayswater Road or Victoria Street. One reason may well have been the hostility of the 'carriage-folk', at least in the case of Bayswater Road. Incidentally, the well-known picture of a large double-deck tram at the Marble Arch is completely imaginary.

Train next tried his luck in Darlington where his trams ran for three years (1862-4) but again the use of the step-rail resulted in the compulsory removal of the line. During the same years Train was also running the Staffordshire Potteries Street Railway Co. from Hanley to Burslem. In 1864, grooved rails replaced the step rails and the tramway thenceforward had a prosperous career until, long after conversion to mechanical traction, it was overwhelmed by a flood of motorbuses in the 1920s.

Far-away Sydney in Australia started horse trams in December, 1861 but they were unpopular and were suspended after five years.

Growing traffic between the mainland and the Isle of Wight prompted the first Act of Parliament for

Left: Having pulled the car uphill, these mules were allowed to ride on the way down

Below left: Bristol's first tram standing in Maudlin Street, 1875

Below: Metropolitan Street tram on the Westminster Bridge - Kennington route, opened in 1870

Bottom: Rival conductors in this contemporary cartoon battle for the custom of the fat lady and her child

a public street tramway in the United Kingdom. The Landport and Southsea Tramway Company was authorized in 1863 to lay a line from Portsmouth Town Station to Clarence Pier, a distance of a little over a mile. It was opened in 1865 with grooved rails and a gauge of 4ft. 7¾in., this being chosen so that ordinary railway wagons or carriages could use it. Though there is no evidence that in fact they did so, this non-standard measurement remained Portsmouth's choice until the end of tramway operation in 1936. Before this line came into use on the mainland a horse tramway was opened, in 1864, along the lengthy Ryde Pier on the other side of Spithead. A similar horse tramway had operated along the pier at Southend, Essex from 1846.

These lines were built specially for the convenience of boat passengers. To Liverpool goes the honour of securing the first Act of Parliament for a local tramway service. The Liverpool Tramways Co. got its Act in 1868 and started operations in November, 1869, using 16 cars built in New York, appropriately enough by John Stephenson. The cars were 46-seat double-deckers.

Before this trams had started in Copenhagen in 1863, in Berlin and Vienna in 1865, in Hamburg in

SHE DECEIVED HER JOHNNY,
THE KEW BUS AND THE INCUBUS.

COMPOSED BY
WALTER REDMOND, ✦ HARRY HUNTER,
SUNG WITH THE GREATEST SUCCESS BY THE
MOHAWK MINSTRELS,
(AGRICULTURAL HALL, LONDON.)
LONDON;
HOPWOOD & CREW, 42, NEW BOND ST W.

Below: A 70 year-old interurban car still in service on the
Manx Electric Railway, in the station at Douglas, Isle of Man

Bottom: A 1900 tram car from Lisbon, employed latterly for
tourist trips round the city

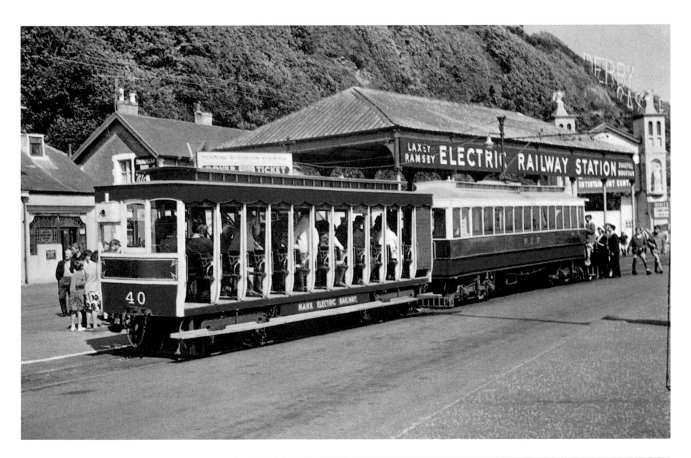

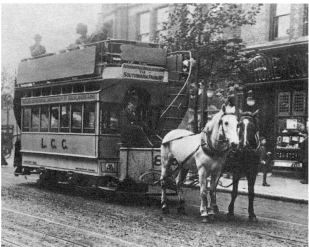

1866 and in Brussels in 1869 also. The first Berlin tram, a double-decker, with Gothic windows on the lower deck and an awning over the open top deck, has been preserved. Berlin was an ideal city for trams in the sense that its most rapid period of growth occurred when Prussia became the acknowledged head of the German Confederation after the defeat and exclusion of Austria from it in 1866. The many new streets were wide and often built with tramway reservations from the start. Unfortunately the authorities exercised little planning control and far too many competitive lines were allowed.

By contrast, competing bus services in Berlin were compulsorily amalgamated in 1868 into the Allgemeine Berliner Omnibus Aktiengesellschaft, usually known as ABOAG, and this had a continuous existence until 1929.

The famous orator, John Bright, who was a keen supporter of trams, became President of the Board of Trade in 1868 and it was probably through his influence that in the following year three companies were incorporated by Act of Parliament and authorized to build street tramways. They were the North Metropolitan, the Metropolitan Street and the Pimlico, Peckham and Greenwich Street Tramways. Dur-

Right: One of Thomas Tilling's extensive chain of South London buses

Centre: South London horse cars at North Street terminus, Wandsworth

Below: Off for a day in the country on a four-horse brake

ing the parliamentary proceedings reference was made to the street railways in the United States already mentioned and also to others in Valparaiso, Havana, Vera Cruz, Mexico City, Copenhagen, Geneva and Brussels.

The Metropolitan Street began a service from Brixton to Kennington Church on May 2nd, 1870 and exactly a week later, the North Metropolitan opened a route from Whitechapel Church to Bow Church. The Pimlico, Peckham and Greenwich did not begin its service until December 13th, 1870 when cars began to run between New Cross and Blackheath Hill.

From then on the tram began to take an increasing share of the passenger traffic on the London streets. By the end of the century it was dominant in south and east London but it was excluded from the heart of the City proper and from the West End. It quickly became in the popular mind a working-class vehicle and, as the century progressed, this image became more firmly fixed as the tramway operators undertook the responsibility of providing cars at low fares for 'artisans, mechanics and day labourers'. They soon began working in the morning long before the buses were out and as early as January, 1899 the North Metropolitan

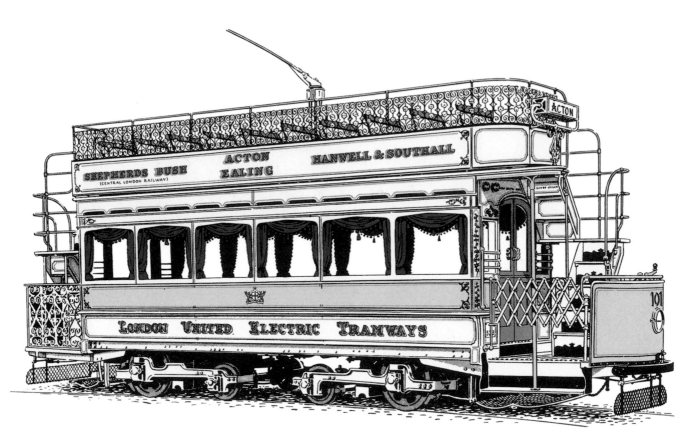

Above left: London United X-class car of 1901 showing scroll work of the period, reproduced from *Tramcyclopaedia* by Vernon E. Prescott-Pickup (Prescott-Pickup & Co. Ltd)

Below left: Photographed in 1962, this Glasgow tram had been in service for nearly fifty years

Above: The B-type bus which put the London General on its feet, reproduced from *Early Buses and Trams* by David Trussler (Hugh Evelyn)

Below: Bristol tram built in 1900 which remained in service until the system closed in 1941

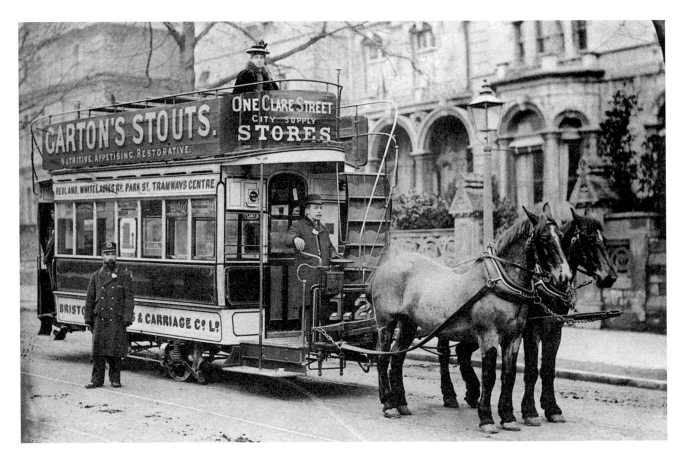

started an all-night service. The idea that the tram was a working-class vehicle seems to have been peculiar to London. In the provinces it was usually more warmly received, especially in later years when electricity became the motive power.

The last horse tramway to be opened in the London area was the single route of the South-East Metropolitan from Greenwich to Rushey Green, brought into service in 1891. By that time on the south side of the river the lines also reached Wandsworth (by two routes), Tooting, Streatham Hill, Tulse Hill, Greenwich and (with a break of gauge) Plumstead. Lines in Croydon were quite separate from the London network.

There was no line across any of the bridges but there was an isolated route in Vauxhall Bridge Road. There were short routes from Shepherds Bush and Hammersmith westwards and other isolated lines from Kew Bridge to Richmond and in Harrow Road. In north and east London the main arteries were served and routes stretched to Wood Green, Ponders End and Leytonstone. Leyton had another isolated system.

In the London area, in 1898, there were 147 miles of street with tram lines, served by 1,451 cars. The horses employed numbered 13,954 and £3,916,556

had been invested in the 16 undertakings which owned this network. Of these the London County Council did not become an operator until the following year. An odd man out was the Highgate Hill cable line to which reference will be made in the next chapter. Passengers carried during the year numbered 309 millions. This figure does not include the Croydon system for which no statistics are available. In the same year the buses carried about 280 million. Where trams were introduced they almost drove the buses off the road.

Many experiments were carried out with various forms of mechanical traction in the 1870s and '80s but in London the horse was certainly supreme until after 1900, for in addition to the expansion of tramway services the horse bus services developed, too, in the districts unserved by trams. It was much the same in the provinces and in other countries.

The dominant position of the London General Omnibus Co. was challenged in 1881 by the appearance of the London Road Car Co., which put a new type of vehicle on the road, with a platform and proper staircase to the top deck. At first platform, stairs, and entrance to the lower deck were in front but these were soon moved to the rear. At the same

time 'garden' seats, i.e. transverse seats each seating two, were introduced on top in place of the 'knifeboard'. So emerged the 26-seater bus which became standard in the last two decades of horse operation. One result of the competition from the Road Car Co. was the wide introduction of 1d. fares on the buses.

The associations continued until the end of horse bus operation but many other operators started after the Road Car Co. so that the London General had a difficult time in the closing years of the century, as it also had to compete with new suburban and underground railway services.

Development of the tram in Great Britain, after the early services had started, was controlled by the Tramways Act, 1870, which in later years had a stultifying effect on expansion and improvement. It compelled tramway owners to maintain the roadway between the rails and for 18 inches on either side. This was bad enough when the operator was also the road authority; it became an intolerable burden when the two were not the same body. The Act also gave local authorities an absolute veto on new routes and this weapon was often used to extort unreasonable concessions from promoters. Moreover, all newly constructed lines were subject to compulsory

purchase by local authorities after 21 years from their opening, so that private operators had little encouragement to improve their efficiency.

Nevertheless the Tramways Act was followed by a spate of promotions. Horse trams started in Edinburgh and Leeds in 1871, in Glasgow, the Black Country and Plymouth in 1872, in Leicester in 1874 and then in most of the big centres.

There was an ingenious attempt about 1861 to improve on Loubat's tram-bus. A bus proprietor in Pendleton (now part of Salford), named John Greenwood, got permission to operate a route on 'Haworth's patent perambulating system', from Broad Street, Pendleton to Albert Bridge on the border of Salford and Manchester. Tracks were laid in the roadway, which differed from those previously built, as in addition to the normal running rails there was a grooved rail placed centrally between them. The vehicles used on the service were apparently ordinary knifeboard buses but, suspended from the body was a rod at the end of which was a guide wheel. This ran in the centre groove, so keeping the outer wheels on the running rails. Where the track ended the 'perambulator' could be retracted and the vehicle continued as a normal bus.

Class C1 M.E.T. car built in 1908, pictured after its adaptation for through running with L.C.C. but before the top cover was fitted, reproduced from *Tramcyclopaedia* by Vernon E. Prescott-Pickup (Prescott-Pickup & Co. Ltd)

MECHANICAL MARVELS

As railroads spread in America, it became not at all uncommon to see locomotives puffing along town streets, especially in the newer areas developing far beyond the Atlantic seaboard, but these were not, of course, intended for local service. On the continent of Europe, particularly in the west, many secondary lines were developed which ran on their own reservations in the country and in town streets, but very few similar lines were ever constructed in the British Isles.

The application of steam to purely urban transport involved considerable difficulties since, to placate public opinion, locomotive designers had to provide machines which were silent, emitted no smoke and had no exposed parts which might endanger the safety of pedestrians and horses.

Although Philadelphia had half a dozen steam cars working in 1860, American inventors preferred to turn their attention to other forms of traction and the steam tram never became so important in North America as it did in Europe or Australasia.

Generally it was found more practicable to operate separate locomotives drawing trailers rather than self-contained units. Many of the latter were tried, however, including Britain's first steam tram. This was John Grantham's car, built by Merryweather and Sons, which in November, 1873 made trial runs in Vauxhall Bridge Road, London and in 1876 was used to open the Wantage Tramway, one of England's few roadside lines. Although the Wantage tramway ceased to carry passengers in 1925, it continued as a goods line for another twenty years.

In 1876 also, steam was used on the newly constructed Southern Tramways of Paris and in the two following years on some of the Northern company's routes but steam operation in Paris was not continuous. Its use on the Southern route, Gare Montparnasse—Place Valhubert is important since the vehicles used were the first 'dummy' locomotives (i.e. independent of carriages) to be put into service. They were designed by another Englishman, G. P. Harding, and also built by Merryweather.

Steam dummies were also built in England to the design of Henry Hughes of Falcon Works, Loughborough from 1876 onwards and thus began a long connection of those works with road transport. They

Above: Steam car experiments for urban transport were carried out on both sides of the Atlantic although steam trams were to prove more popular in Europe and Australasia. This car was one of eight which were tried out in Bristol in 1880-1

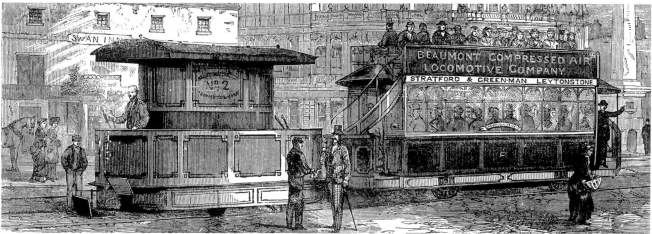

passed eventually into the hands of the Brush Engineering Co., and became famous as builders, first of electric trams and then of motor buses. Their badge, the falcon, is still to be seen on vehicles today.

Engines by Hughes worked on the first British steam tramway entirely in town streets—the Vale of Clyde, whose lines in Govan (now part of Glasgow) were opened in 1877. During the 1880s, steam was adopted extensively for tramways in the industrial Midlands of England, the West Riding of Yorkshire and parts of Lancashire, with isolated services elsewhere. From 1885 to 1891 steam trams ran from the London county boundary at Finsbury Park to Wood Green and Ponders End.

The opening of one steam tramway system—that of Huddersfield in 1883—had an important effect on transport history in the British Isles, not because of the form of traction used, but because Huddersfield was the first municipality to become an operator. This was quite by chance. Huddersfield laid several

miles of track and then could not find anyone to lease the system. The corporation therefore obtained parliamentary powers to work the lines itself.

The general rule in Britain was to have one trailer only and large double-deck cars on two bogies seating about 60 became standard. The largest of all was a car 44ft. long and seating 100, built for the Wolverton and Stony Stratford tramway in Buckinghamshire. This line lasted until 1926, when the staff joined in the General Strike of that year, the service stopped abruptly and was never restarted. Most British steam tramways were converted to electricity before 1910.

Sydney, Australia had steam cars from 1879 to 1937 and Christchurch, New Zealand until 1912, with some still working as peak hour extras until 1925.

The prohibition on more than one trailer which was usual in Great Britain did not apply across the Channel and many hundreds of miles of light railway were constructed on the continent to provide both passenger and goods services.

One of the earliest of these roadside lines to use steam was the tramway from Rueil to Marley-le-Roi, north-west of Paris, which was reconstructed from a primitive horse tramway and opened in 1878 using

Top: Thomson's road steamer on trial between Edinburgh and Leith, 1870

Above: The Beaumont compressed-air engine seen running at Stratford, Essex, 1881

'fireless' locomotives. Designed by an American, Dr Lamm, and improved by a Frenchman named Francq, these ingenious engines were driven by super-charged steam and, therefore, had the disadvantage of needing a recharge at the end of each journey. Nevertheless they seem to have worked successfully for many years.

It was in Belgium that the idea of a network of secondary lines connecting all the principal parts of the country together was most enthusiastically taken up and developed. The creation of the Société Nationale des Chemins de Fer Vicinaux in 1884

Right: Blackpool and Lytham gas tram, 1896

Centre: Cable car and dummy in Melbourne

Below: Chicago cable car and trailer on the Blue Island route, 1895

gave the country a unified network of steam light railways which in many cases became in effect extensions of town tramways. In ten years 1,250 km. of lines were constructed and by 1913, 4,094 km. were in service. But this is running too far ahead.

Coming back to Paris, steam 'dummies' were not favoured for services within the fortifications, and self-contained vehicles (automotrices) to the designs of Rowan, Serpollet and Purrey were employed. Some of these continued to work until 1914.

The objection to steam in urban streets and the uncertainties of electricity until nearly the end of

Left: Kitson steam engine and trailer on the Birmingham and Midland tramways, 1897

Right: Steam engine and trailer with crew, 1886

Bottom: Scene at the opening of one of Britain's few rural tramways, the Alford and Sutton steam line in Lincolnshire, on April 2, 1884

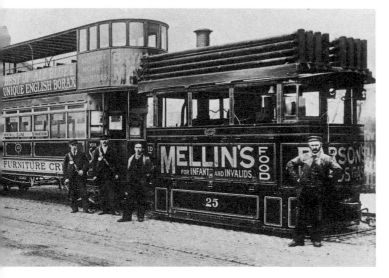

the nineteenth century led to many experiments, of which Paris had a fair share. One of these was with the use of compressed air on Mekarski's system. Only in France was a regular service of any duration established using this form of traction. Mekarski cars were tried in Caledonian Road, London in 1883 and 1885, and a regular service was run for about four months in 1888. After Nantes had started using compressed air in 1879, Mekarski cars were put to work in Nogent-sur-Marne in 1887. Eventually, according to the researches of M. Jean Robert, some 208 Mekarski cars were employed in the Paris area

and the majority of these lasted until 1913-14. It was necessary to warm the air with steam before admitting it to the driving cylinders and this caused the engines to produce a chuffing sound when in motion which might lead the uninitiated to suppose they were steamers, especially as a large hot-water boiler was mounted on the front platform. Apart from this chuffing the Mekarski cars were fairly silent and could pull heavy trailers on reasonable gradients, in addition to their own loads, but they suffered from two defects—the necessity to recharge frequently and the unreliability of their air-brakes.

Top: Behind the ice-cream man at the Place du Châtelet, Paris—a Mekarski compressed-air tram and a horse bus with 'knifeboard' seating on the top deck

Bottom: A contemporary engraving illustrating Hallidie's patent cable system

A more practical substitute for horse power was cable traction. Paris only had one example of this, the short and rather misnamed Belleville funicular; it was in the United States that the cable-car was most warmly welcomed. As most readers will know, cable-cars still run in San Francisco and are regarded as one of the city's sights, as well as being an efficient means of transport on steep gradients. The idea of hauling vehicles by an endless rope wound round pulleys at each end of the track, with the pulleys driven by steam power, was a fairly obvious one but the difficulty was to find a quick method for detaching and reattaching the vehicles to the cable. W. J. Curtis, whom we have met before, devised a quick release gripper as long ago as 1838, but it was a San Francisco wire-rope manufacturer, Andrew S. Hallidie, who built the first street railway worked by cable traction.

Hallidie risked the whole of his capital (and some other people's) to construct a line on Clay Street, a hill with a 1 in 5 gradient in places. The cable was put underground below a slot centrally placed between the running rails. From the car through the slot passed a long rod which could be turned to bring the faces of the gripper into contact with the cable.

When Hallidie's line started on August 1st, 1873 it was an immediate success and was widely copied in America. Chicago, Philadelphia, Washington, New York, Denver, St Louis, Kansas City and other places all had large cable systems by the 1890s. The Chicago cables, the most extensive in the world, lasted until 1906.

Despite a very high initial cost, cablecars proved cheaper to run than horsecars and they could carry much heavier loads, but they always operated under the shadow of a possible break in the cable. When this did happen, there was no knowing how long the service might be stopped. Curves, junctions and crossings over other lines presented formidable difficulties and their negotiation called for a very nice judgement on the part of gripmen, as the drivers soon came to be called. Speed, too, was necessarily low.

Very few examples of cable traction (apart from cliff lifts and the like) were to be found in Great Britain and only one survives—the Great Orme Tramway at Llandudno, which has a street section and also runs across open country. There were two lines in London. One was on Highgate Hill, opened in 1884, and the other a longer line from Kennington

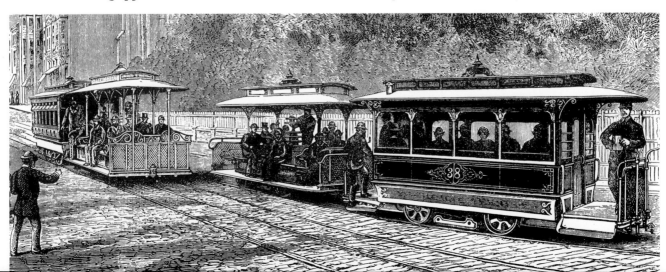

to Streatham opened in 1892. Birmingham, Matlock and Douglas also had short lines. The biggest British system was in Edinburgh, started at the late date of 1888 and continued until 1922. It employed 205 double-deck cars.

The last cable system of any size was that in Melbourne, Australia, started in 1885. At its peak it employed over 1,200 cars and trailers and had 46 miles of double track. The last car did not run until 1940. Sydney also had cable cars from 1884 to 1905.

Less successful were some of the other mechanical marvels tried out from 1870 onwards. Ammonia gas was tried in New Orleans. Cars were built both in England and America which were worked by springs, like gigantic clockwork toys. Another cranky idea was a stern wheel with feet which would push a car along as the driver wound a hand wheel on the front platform.

There were, too, early internal combustion engines of which the best known was the Connelly, using naphtha, which was tried both in London and New York in the '80s and '90s. Town gas was successfully used to drive trams at Lytham-St Anne's and in Trafford Park, England and Neath, South Wales, the latter system lasting until 1920.

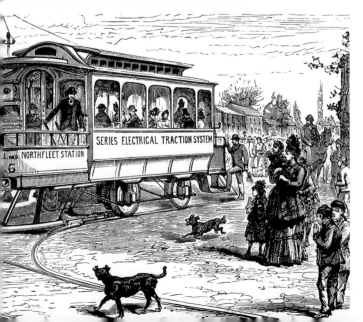

It was electricity that made the tram the supreme vehicle for urban mass transportation on the highway. Early experiments relied on the use of batteries and it was not until the dynamo was invented and perfected that electric traction became really practicable. The success of Werner von Siemens in working a reliable electric locomotive at the Berlin Industrial Exhibition in 1879 really started a new era.

On May 16th, 1881, Siemens started the first public electric service from the station at Lichterfelde, near Berlin to the Anhalt Cadet School 1½ miles away. The only trouble with this was the danger in using the running rails as current conductors and many experiments were made both in Europe and America to find something safer.

A Kansas farmer, J. C. Henry, invented a 'troller', two wheels running on wires above the track and connected by wires to the motor in the car but he had difficulty in controlling the current. In the same year, 1884, an early form of conduit with the wires under the surface and reached through a slot like those on the cable lines, was tried in Cleveland, Ohio. To the inventors of this, E. M. Bentley and W. H. Page, we owe the word 'plow' (in England, 'plough') for the collector which made the contact.

43

Left: Reckenzaun's battery electric car at Kew, Middlesex, 1883

Centre: Lifu steam car and canopied trailer at Portsmouth about 1900

Below: Daimler's benzine tram at Cannstatt, 1887

Recent researches by A. Winstan Bond and G. B. Claydon have brought to light the story of Henry Block Binko. After the Siemens system had been demonstrated at the Crystal Palace, London in 1881, Binko installed a 20-inch gauge line at the Palace which seems to have worked intermittently in 1882-4. Then he appeared in Edinburgh giving demonstrations at the Forestry Exhibition in the grounds of Donaldson's Hospital. His little train drawn by a small electric locomotive was patronized by the Prince and Princess of Wales and later by Mr and Mrs Gladstone. After this success he obtained permission to equip about 700 yards of the existing horse track from outside the exhibition to the Haymarket railway station by laying two strips of copper plate between the running rails and taking current from them by a wheeled collector under the car.

While these and other experiments were going on three lines were started in the British Isles which definitely proved the practicability of electric traction. Magnus Volk started a 2ft. 8½in. gauge electric railway along Brighton Promenade on August 4th, 1883 and it still runs every summer. On September 18th, 1883, the Giant's Causeway, Portrush and Bush Valley Railway and Tramway Co., started

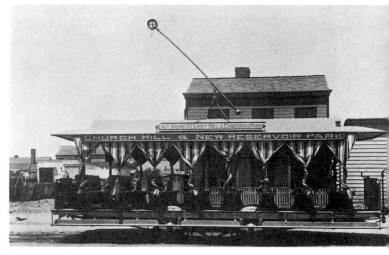

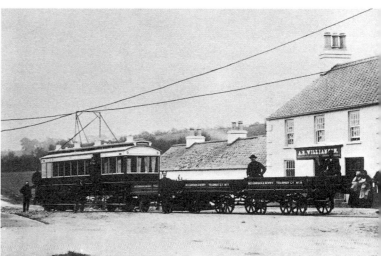

Right: Frank J. Sprague's car with trolley wheel in Richmond, Virginia, 1887

Centre: In Ireland the Bessbrook and Newry Tramway used a bow collector for crossing roads; ordinary carts were towed for goods

Below: E. Van Depoele's motor on the platform of a car at Wheeling, West Virginia, 1887

operation on the first portion of its line in Northern Ireland. Inspired by two brothers, W. A. and Anthony Traill with the aid of C. W. Siemens, this line was the first in the world to use hydro-electric generation. It lasted until 1949. Also in Ireland was the Bessbrook and Newry Tramway opened in October, 1885. Like the Giant's Causeway line and Volk's (after initial use of the running rails), the Bessbrook and Newry used a third rail for current collection. It also had the unusual features of a bow collector on the motor-cars contacting an overhead wire where it crossed public roads and a device enabling ordinary four-wheeled horse-carts to be towed as part of a train.

Shortly before the Bessbrook and Newry opened, a conduit tramway started in Blackpool on September 29th, 1885. It was designed by Michael Holroyd Smith and, despite a good deal of trouble through sand and seawater getting into the slot, operated with a few interruptions until 1899, when the overhead system replaced the conduit.

It took some years for inventors in America to evolve a thoroughly reliable and workable electric car. Leo Daft, a Briton, and C. J. van Depoele, a Belgian, had partial success using either the running

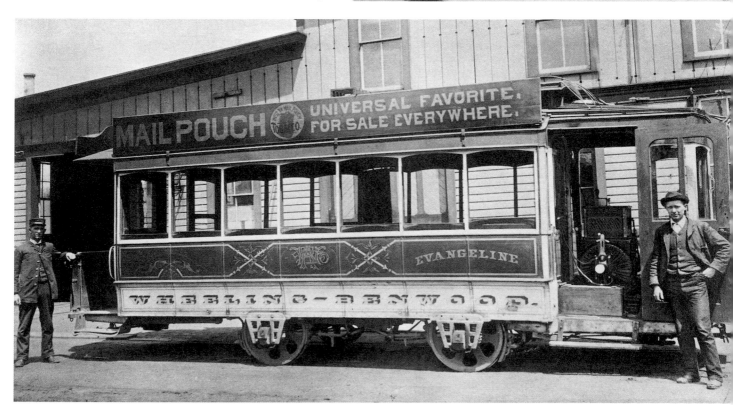

Below: The first overhead trolley line in Britain, installed at
Leeds in 1891

Right: An East Oakland, California double-decker at Indian
Gulch, 1894

Below right: The driver and conductor of a Bloxwich tram at
Wednesbury, Staffordshire, 1899

rails for the current or overhead 'trollers'. But the
man whose work more than any other was responsible
for the triumph of the electric streetcar was Frank
Julian Sprague, who used and improved the now
familiar trolley-pole instead of the 'troller' for collection, designed a mounting for the motors that
kept the gearing between them and the road wheels
in constant mesh, showed that regenerative braking
(i.e. reversing the motors so that they become gene-
rators) was practicable and above all invented multiple-unit control, which, while not generally applica-
ble to street-car operation, made possible the electrical operation of heavy interurban and underground
railways.

Despite tremendous difficulties, Sprague provided
Richmond, Virginia with an electric street-railway
system which began public service on February 2nd,
1888 and was an instantaneous success. Electric lines
began to spring up all over America and in Germany
and Italy. At the end of the century the United States
had more than 15,000 miles of electrified track and
the urban lines were beginning to stretch out to link
individual communities together.

A most interesting development was the building
of tunnels to avoid congested streets in the centre of
Boston. The Tremont Street Subway was opened
in 1897; it was the scene in 1901-9 of an unusual
operating arrangement, when it accommodated both
normal street cars and the trains of the Elevated
Railway which dived into and out of it from and to
their superstructure above the streets. It is odd that
the subway was not more widely used in large cities
as a normal part of street car operation. Only in
the last few years, when the tram has disappeared
from most countries, has there been really practical
interest in putting the trams underground in some
major cities of Europe.

The British Isles were much slower to adopt
electric traction in spite of the early and successful
examples already quoted. For some years interest
was shown in battery operation, the most notable
inventor in this field being Anthony Reckenzaun, an
Austrian who settled in England. The use of accumulators ceased to have any point as current trans-
mission became more reliable but Reckenzaun's
work had some important lasting effects for he showed
(in advance of his time) the practicability of series-
parallel control and the advantages of using bogie
trucks with the bulk of the weight on the driven axles.
He also invented a combined hand and electric brake

in which current was used to magnetize the brake blocks. Battery cars worked regularly along Barking Road, West Ham from 1889 to 1892 and on Bristol Road, Birmingham from 1890 to 1901. Third-rail lines on Ryde Pier (1886) and Southend Pier (1890) survived for many years but an experiment with a conduit installation at Gravesend in 1889 was not a success.

Progress can really be dated from October 29th, 1891 when the 2½ mile Roundhay tramway in Leeds was officially opened, with public transport beginning on November 11th. It took current from overhead wires and used a trolley pole with wheel to collect it. The engineer, William Graff-Baker, was American and so were the original small single-deck cars, supplied appropriately enough by the firm founded by John Stephenson.

Bradford, never to be outdone by Leeds, tried in 1892 a remarkable car designed partly by M. Holroyd Smith and partly by Reckenzaun. It was a double-decker employing four motors with worm-drive and having both regenerative and slipper brakes. Unfortunately the then high cost of current killed this experiment. In the same year the Guernsey Railway electrified its roadside tramway.

Before the beginning of the 20th century electric trams were running in Walsall (1893), Bristol and Coventry (1895), Dublin (1896), Dover (1897), Cork, Glasgow and Liverpool (1898), Aberdeen, Blackburn, the Potteries and Sheffield (1899) and Darwen, Dundee, Southampton, Sunderland and Swansea (1900). The capital lagged behind and what happened there must be told in the next chapter.

Paris was almost as slow as London to take advantage of electric traction. As in London, battery traction was first tried and worked for several years on some northern routes, but was very unpopular because of the fumes from the accumulators which were placed under the seats.

The next development was in the eastern suburb of Romainville which from June 1st, 1896 was linked with the Place de la République by a tramway drawing current from a closed conduit, that is, on what came to be known as the stud system. Every 2½ metres along the centre of the track between the running rails was a metal stud projecting 5mm. above the paving. When a skate, mounted under a car, passed over these they became live and fed current to the car motors. In practice there was often trouble as the studs remained live after a car had passed, with unpleasant results for pedestrians and horses. Despite this, studs were used on several other lines in Paris for seven or eight years.

There was strong opposition to overhead wires inside the fortifications and although some suburban lines adopted this system from 1895 onwards it was well into the twentieth century before its use became general in central Paris. Some early cars were dual-equipped using trolley poles outside the walls and accumulators inside. The important route Bastille – Charenton was electrified on the dual system of overhead on the outskirts and conduit in the centre of the city, while the cars on Villemomble – Place de

Left: What might have been: artist's impression of the possible effects of motor traction, 1898

Below left: Coventry's first electric car which was put into service in 1895

Below: Cross country car seen near Grenoble, France

Right: De Dion articulated bus, Paris, 1898

Below right: 12-seater De Dion bus, 1898

Bottom: On a smaller scale—Benz 8-seater hotel bus, 1895

THE DION 'BUS FOR THIRTY PERSONS

la République could operate on overhead or conduit or by accumulator.

The biggest of the companies which provided street transport in Paris and its environs at the end of the nineteenth century, la Compagnie Générale des Omnibus, alone had done nothing towards electrification. With all the bus routes and many central tram routes in its hands it had no incentive to expend capital in changing, especially as its concession was due to expire in 1910.

We have already referred to the pioneer work of von Siemens, which led in the '80s to a great expansion of electric tramways in Germany, Switzerland and Austria, helped (in Germany, at any rate) by the law permitting municipalities to invest in companies and by the way in which joint purchasing and research were introduced at an early date.

Budapest had a conduit system (with the slot in one of the running rails) from 1889 and Berlin had one from 1896. Berlin also used battery-driven cars from 1894. These were equipped for overhead current collection as well and could take current to charge their batteries while running.

Austria, Belgium, Holland, Italy, Spain and Portugal as well as Australia, the Argentine and South Africa all had electric trams before 1901 and it was a fair deduction that urban transport in the future would depend entirely on this form of vehicle.

But progress in refining towards the end of the nineteenth century led to the production of petroleum spirit or gasoline. The Germans, Gottlieb Daimler and Karl Benz, both proved the practicability of petrol-driven vehicles in 1885 and French inventors followed them in producing a number of early automobiles. Great Britain was well behind but, thanks largely to R. F. Simms, Daimler rights were secured and manufacture started at Coventry.

In the '80s and '90s several experiments with steam, electric and petrol buses were made in London. One of these promised to become permanent but even that failed. Two vehicles with German Daimler engines, belonging to the Motor Traction Co. Ltd., worked from October 9th, 1899 to December, 1900, first between Kennington and Victoria via Westminster and then between Kennington and Oxford Circus.

When those vehicles were withdrawn London, like all the other great cities of the world, found herself at the start of the twentieth century without a single motor bus in service.

END OF AN ERA

The early years of the twentieth century brought an electric traction mania which, in North America, meant not only a proliferation of street lines but the creation of several great networks of interurban light railways. These operated tramway-type vehicles which were heavier, faster and usually more comfortable than the local streetcar. Their routes were almost always along town streets in the built-up areas and then on private rights-of-way. Current collection was usually by trolley pole from an overhead wire and cars were more often operated singly than in trains. Speeds of fifty to sixty miles an hour on the reservations were common and up to eighty was not unknown.

Passengers were more important to most lines than freight, although many companies performed a very useful function in acting as carriers for isolated rural communities. It must be remembered that at this time, relative to the size of those countries, both the United States and Canada had a very small mileage of reasonable roads outside the towns, so that rail service was a great boon.

In so many instances did land values soar that many interurbans were planned with the deliberate object of creating profits for land speculators.

Interurbans were mainly constructed in two great bursts of activity, 1901-4 and 1905-8 with a financial crisis in between. They reached their maximum mileage of 15,580 in 1916; this was an official figure which largely ignored many lines in New England which were definitely prolongations of street railways although they linked independent communities.

Ohio with 2,798 miles had the greatest interurban mileage and the adjoining states of Indiana (1,825 miles), Pennsylvania (1,498); Illinois (1,422) and Michigan (981) were high on the list. Most of the Pennsylvania mileage, however, was in the east. The Illinois systems too, were quite separate but the lines in Michigan, Indiana and Ohio connected at a number of points and large areas of these states were covered. From 1910 to 1922 it would have been possible, if one had had the time, to travel by interurban from Elkhart Lake in eastern Wisconsin to Oneonta, in the centre of New York State, a distance of 1,087 miles.

Although the greater part of the interurban mileage in both the United States and Canada had been abandoned before the Second World War, many lines in Iowa held on much longer, mainly because they developed substantial freight business in contrast

Left: In 1903 the Eastbourne Corporation brought a number of Milnes-Daimler buses into service

Below: Opening day of the electric tramway at Port Elizabeth, South Africa, 1897

Bottom: This swivel-top tower mounted on a horse-drawn cart was used by engineers in the early 1900s to maintain the overhead electric wires

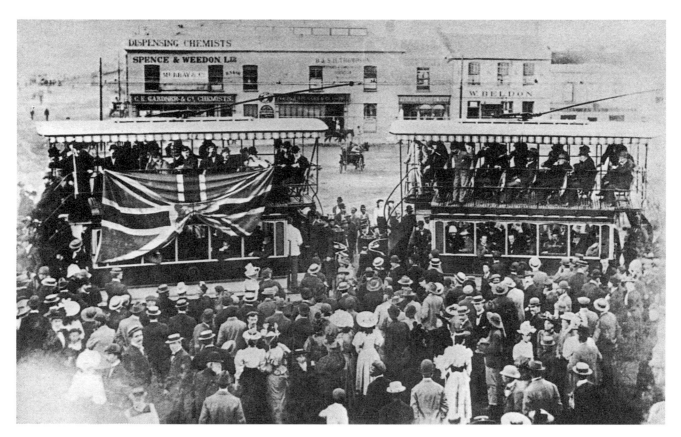

to the lines further east. Texas, oddly enough, built most of its interurbans after 1910, when construction in other states had almost ceased. (By a coincidence, too, if we may jump many years ahead, it was in Texas that the last completely new tramway was built in the States—a short line about ¾-mile long to serve a large store in Fort Worth.) California had the notable Pacific Electric Railway which eventually owned over 700 route miles.

Canada had about 850 miles of interurban, more than half in Ontario (where they were called 'radials') but most of the systems were isolated.

Usually the interurbans terminated in city steets but some had special terminus buildings, the largest being the Indianapolis Traction Terminal with nine tracks and a nine-storey office block. At Baltimore there was an interesting terminal with six tracks sited within a loop road. Los Angeles Main Street terminal had seven tracks for passengers plus a large freight depot.

Britain had nothing comparable to the American network although some of the earliest electric lines in the United Kingdom were of interurban character. Reference has already been made to the Giants' Causeway and the Bessbrook and Newry lines. The

Top: London trolleybus no. 1, commonly known as 'the diddler', built in 1931, at the Fulwell Depot

Bottom: London buses in Oxford Street, 1962

Top: Modern Paris buses with automatic doors

Bottom: Rear view of an older-style 'bull nose' bus in Paris

Manx Electric opened in 1894 and still running, also resembles an American interurban, especially as it has only short lengths in the public roadway.

The Blackpool and Fleetwood Tramway (also still in existence as part of the Blackpool Corporation system) is clearly an interurban; it was opened in 1896. The Burton and Ashby Light Railway, ten miles long, was built by the Midland Railway in 1906 as an alternative to an orthodox steam line but only about a mile was across fields. The Grimsby and Immingham, with a mile of street track in Grimsby and a short length in Immingham but otherwise running by the side of a steam line, was part of the Great Central Railway plan for developing Immingham in 1912. There was, of course, the Swansea – Mumbles but this was not electrified until 1929.

There were a number of other places where electric trams connected towns or villages with a mixture of street and cross-country or roadside running such as the Dunfermline District system in Fife, the Tyneside Tramways and Tramroads Company's Wallsend – Gosforth line, the Kinver Light Railway in South Staffordshire, the Kidderminster and Stourport in Worcestershire, the Isle of Thanet routes, the Portsdown and Horndean in Hampshire, the Llandudno

and Colwyn Bay in North Wales and the Dublin and Lucan in Ireland.

This was about all that could be compared in any way with the American interurbans and they all (except the Grimsby and Immingham and the Kinver) at some time or other ran double-deckers, which no American interurban ever did.

The British pattern was much more one of town services being extended into the surrounding countryside as the built-up area was pushed out, or of lines reaching out from neighbouring towns until they touched. Physical contact did not always lead to through running for one of the curses of tramway operation in Britain was the excessive parochialism fostered by the Act of 1870.

Local authorities were able to hold promoters to ransom and where they intended to operate themselves, instead of leasing, often took decisions which made through running impossible. This was particularly the case in the West Riding of Yorkshire. As an example the eleven miles from Bradford to Huddersfield was covered by three undertakings. Bradford had six miles on 4ft. gauge, Halifax a little over one mile on 3ft. 6in. gauge and Huddersfield the remainder on 4ft. 7¾in. gauge.

Left: A view of Market Street, Newark, New Jersey in about 1909, showing a line of trolleys but not a single automobile

Below and right: Pittsburgh-Butler interurban equipped with a trolley pole for town use and a pantograph for cross-country working

Bottom: A postal and passenger car from Boston, U.S.A.

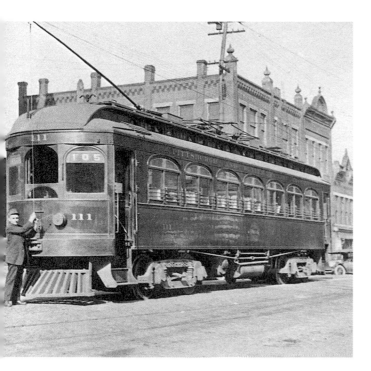

Below: The great shed formed only a part of the Indianapolis
terminal building which was the largest of its kind in the U.S.A.

In colour: Two views of the tramway system in Dubrovnik

Direct operation by a· municipality was, until relatively recent years, a peculiarly British institution. In America local authorities gave franchises for a period of years in return for payment of some sort but rarely even constructed the tracks. On the continent of Europe track constructed by local authorities and leased to concessionaires was the most common method. In Belgium as we have already noted, much mileage was in the hands of the publicly-owned but commercially-managed S.N.C.V., while in Germany municipal participation in operating companies was common. There were some important undertakings both municipally owned and managed in Austria and Italy but this can be regarded as exceptional.

A great problem in the first decade of the century in many large cities was to avoid waste of capital in the construction of unremunerative competitive lines while at the same time giving the public the best possible service.

Vienna was a good example of controlled planning, encouraged by the lay-out of the city of which the main features are ring and radial roads. Municipalization of the two principal tramway undertakings took place in 1903 and two smaller ones were taken over in 1904 and 1907. The last horse tram ran in 1903.

Until recent years Vienna has been predominantly a tramway city but some motorbuses were introduced on light traffic routes in 1907 and then, in 1913, rather surprisingly, the British Electric Traction group was authorized to run a service of Daimler 34-seat double-deck petrol buses on behalf of the city council. These had a short life in municipal service before the army commandeered them, as it also did the motive power of some horse buses which still survived.

Great use of the tramways was made in the 1914-18 war for the conveyance of freight, even to the extent of hauling ordinary carts behind the motor trams when special vehicles were not available.

Paris was a particularly bad case of development without a plan. Already haphazard, its tramway system was made worse in this respect by a rush to build new lines before the Great Exhibition of 1900 was opened. Some of the routes planned to cope with the expected crowds were not ready in time and were unprofitable from the start.

In 1899, in addition to the short Belleville cable line and two suburban routes on metre gauge, there

were eight companies sharing the street-car traffic in Paris and its immediate environs. In 1900, two of these plus one of the metre gauge lines amalgamated but five new companies appeared and La Compagnie des Tramways Mécaniques des Environs de Paris which, since 1895, had operated an isolated rural line from St. Germain to Poissy, opened lines in some north-western suburbs. The new routes were mostly worked on the overhead system outside the fortifications and on the stud system inside.

Both old and new companies were affected by the opening from 1900 onwards of the Métropolitain, conceived as virtually a fast underground tramway system with frequent stops. One of the new undertakings went bankrupt after only eighteen months and several new routes were quickly abandoned.

The great floods of 1910 did tremendous damage to the permanent way in many quarters and virtually brought to an end operation by studs and accumulators. A general reorganization took place, reducing the number of operators to eleven including the Belleville cable. Most important, the government took a hand. All routes inside the city of Paris were given to the Compagnie Générale des Omnibus while the Département of the Seine was authorized to control

the concessions to the others. All concessions were to terminate on the same day forty years thence, except certain lines in Nogent-sur-Marne.

The omnibus company had begun to experiment with motor buses in 1905 and in the following year converted several routes from horse traction. With the new concession it was able to go ahead with the modernization of both trams and buses. The other companies did the same and by August, 1914, horse-buses, horse-trams, accumulator, compressed air and stud trams had all gone from the streets of Paris. The transformation in so short a time was a great feat of engineering, especially as it involved the construction of a large fleet of new vehicles. It also signalled the end of double-deckers in Paris, as although many ran until the late '20s no more were built.

At five o'clock in the afternoon of August 1st, 1914, all motor bus operation in Paris was stopped. The vehicles were requisitioned for the army or turned into lorries and the trams and the Métro had to handle all the city's traffic until 1916, when some bus routes were restarted.

The situation in London between 1901 and 1914 differed considerably from that in Paris. There was an equally great feat of engineering, for in those few

Bottom: A chance meeting, perhaps, at the Tramways Centre
in Bristol, about 1908

years some 325 miles of road were provided with electric trams. More than half of this was new construction and the work was complicated by the great length that was constructed on the conduit system.

The London County Council took possession of all the lines in the county (except about 5½ miles in Hammersmith and two other short lengths) between 1892 and 1909 and operated them from 1899 onwards. The outlying local authorities of Walthamstow, Leyton, West Ham, East Ham, Ilford, Barking, Erith, Bexley, Dartford and Croydon took over or built tramways in their areas and there were three

company systems, all conducted with great vigour in their early years—the London United, the Metropolitan (most of whose lines were leased from the Middlesex and Hertfordshire County Councils) and the South Metropolitan.

If one ignores an experimental line at the Alexandra Palace in 1898, the credit for opening the first electric car service in the metropolitan area must go to the London United which began operations from Hammersmith and Shepherds Bush on April 4th, 1901, soon followed, on June 22nd, at the other side of London by the East Ham Council's main line.

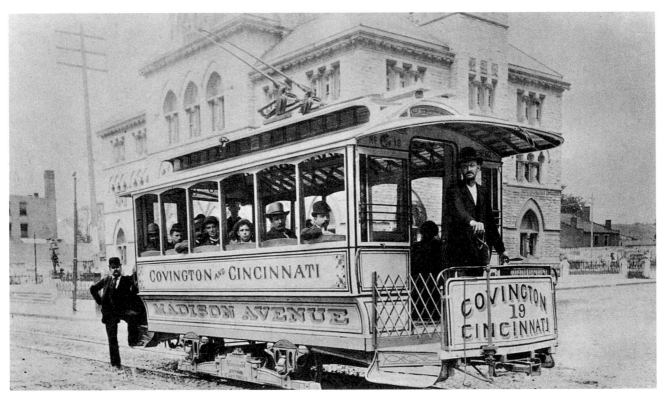

The smaller municipalities were masters in their own houses, but the London United and South Metropolitan companies were continually being frustrated by the short sightedness and greed of the bodies they had to deal with and the L.C.C. itself suffered from the veto which the metropolitan boroughs were able to exercise on the form of traction to be used. This was one of the reasons for the adoption of the expensive conduit and more particularly, for an expensive and unsatisfactory experience with a stud system in Mile End Road in 1908.

Nevertheless the County Council, inspired by the

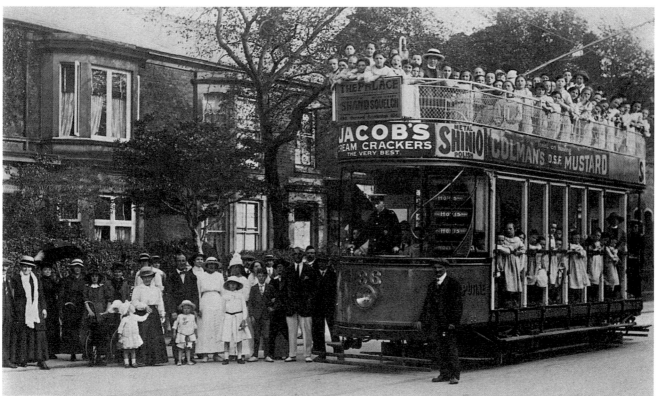

Below: Clarkson steam bus in the fleet of Barton Bros. of Nottingham

Right: Signal box for trams on the horseshoe bend at the top of Colston Street, Bristol

Below right: A Darracq-Serpollet steam bus, operated in London from 1907-12

ideals of public service which animated London's administrators in those days, rapidly built up a network of densely occupied routes at cheap fares, once it started on electrification of the lines south of the Thames in 1903 and north in 1906.

Impressed by the success of the streetcar tunnels in Boston, U.S.A., the council decided to link its northern and southern lines in this way and took advantage of the construction of a new street, Kingsway, to do this. Unfortunately it made the mistake (as it turned out) of building the subway to take single-deck cars only and in 1929-31 it had to be reconstructed at great expense for double-deckers. It was opened partially in 1906 and throughout from Bloomsbury to the Embankment on April 10th, 1908.

In the first decade of the century the trams were hardly challenged in south London but they never served the West End and, in the east, municipal boundaries played right into the hands of the developing motorbus undertakings to which we must now turn our attention.

The new century saw a fresh start with road motor services, first with open wagonettes (small vehicles to seat 8-10 persons). Then in 1902 came a small double-deck Canstatt-Daimler on an outer suburban route (Lewisham – Eltham). In the centre there were experiments with singledeckers, both petrol and steam, in this and the following years.

The firm establishment of the motorbus can be dated from 1904. On September 30th, 1904 Thomas Tilling started a Peckham – Oxford Circus service and on October 11th, Birch Bros. started between Waterloo and Baker Street, later extending to North Finchley. The importance of these services lies not so much in their continuity (the Birch motors were withdrawn in 1908) as in the fact that they employed vehicles specially built as motorbuses—a combined effort by G. F. Milnes & Co. Ltd., a famous tramcar builder, and the German firm of Daimler. The 34-seat double-deck body fitted to these buses was the typical London bus body until after the First World War.

The London General began regular motorbus operation in 1905 and so did the Road Car Co. Both found themselves against a strong new competitor, the London Motor Omnibus Co. Ltd., which adopted the fleet name 'Vanguard'. So rapid was development that whereas 1905 opened with only 20 motorbuses working in London, by July, 1908 there were 1,066.

Competition was exhausting and some combination was inevitable. On July 1st, 1908, the General absorbed the Road Car and Vanguard, so bringing 885 buses into one ownership. An early result of this was the production from 1909 onwards of the General's own buses at Walthamstow, the most famous of these being the 'B' type which entered service in October, 1910 and of which 2,900 in all were built.

The General standardized on petrol, but there were two experiments with vehicles using petrol engines to generate electricity as the motive power and one of these, the Tilling-Stevens, proved extremely successful. Battery-electrics were tried for short periods. Steam appeared effectively in 1907 when the Metropolitan Steam Omnibus Co. Ltd. began running Darracq-Serpollets until the General absorbed it in 1912. The National Steam Car Co. Ltd., using Clarksons, operated in London from 1909 to 1919 and had a maximum fleet of 184.

Another important acquisition by the General was the Great Eastern of London, taken over in 1911, which had made serious inroads into the traffic of the East London municipalities. These had begun interworking between themselves as early as 1904 but the difficulties of through working with the

L.C.C., because of differing traction systems, were not overcome until 1910. From then onwards boundaries diminished in importance.

One of the company tramways, the London United, became associated in 1902 with the Underground Electric Railways of London Ltd. and ten years later the Underground gained control of the General. In 1913 the other two tramway companies also went into what was colloquially called 'the combine'. The smaller bus companies which had not been absorbed by the General by the time the war broke out had working agreements with it, so that all road transport in the metropolitan area was controlled by two groups—the Underground and the municipalities.

One of the smaller undertakings in London was the British Automobile Traction Co., a subsidiary of the British Electric Traction Co., which from the 1890s onwards was busily engaged in building tramways wherever in the country there seemed to be a chance of profitable operation. In 1914 the B.E.T. Co., was still predominantly a tramway concern but it had already begun to experiment with motorbuses in the provinces as well, notably in the Birmingham area and in Durham.

So, too, had many others. The Great Western and the North Eastern Railways both began country bus services in 1903, as did Eastbourne Corporation, the first municipality to do so. From then on services were started in many parts of the country; some soon failed; others became the foundation of the present-day network. Such firms as Southdown Motor Services, Maidstone and District, Crosville and United Automobile Services can all be traced back before 1914.

This was the time of tramway growth throughout the industrial areas of Britain. The tram was predominant wherever there was a concentration of population and outside London and Edinburgh, a

A parade of the early London buses which covered all the main central and suburban routes with their rival networks. Development was most rapid between the years 1905-8 when the number of motorbuses working in London rose from 20 to 1,066. Competition was intense but in time the strength

motorbus was a great rarity. Some tram operators bought one or two buses experimentally, but only as feeders to the tram services. Country places, for the most part, still depended in 1914 on the horse and the railway.

As in America, a number of tramway lines were built which never fulfilled the hopes of their promoters and managements were always seeking to keep costs down and revenue up. While the double-decker, usually on a four-wheel truck for lighter traffic routes and on bogies for the denser routes, became the standard British streetcar, in America and most countries outside the British Empire the single-decker predominated. Curiously enough, thousands of open-sided single-deckers were built in the United States, necessitating in many cases a duplicate fleet. This extravagance had to go and its departure was hastened by the adoption from about 1905 of the 'pay-as-you-enter' system by many undertakings.

It was thought that this would lead to a decrease in fare-evasion but the idea was not altogether successful because of the delays in loading and the additional platform space required. In 1916, Charles O. Birney designed a small four-wheel 'safety' car for one-man operation, but although hundreds were built their vogue only lasted about five years.

Although trailers were used in America much more than in Britain, where they were exceptional, operating them in narrow city streets often presented difficulties and in an effort to overcome these, the Boston Elevated Railway (which as mentioned earlier, also owned a street railway), experimented in 1913 with two old cars between which was hung a central compartment having no wheels of its own but suspended from the two vehicles, so forming an articulated unit. Passengers entered in this middle portion and it was there that the conductor was stationed. It was so successful that more were adapted and were

of the London General began to show and between 1908-12 they had absorbed, among others, the Road Car, Vanguard, Metropolitan and Great Eastern companies, before being themselves absorbed in the same year by the Underground group

part of the Boston scene until 1924. Also in 1913 similar cars appeared in Richmond, Virginia, where they were nicknamed 'two rooms and a bath'.

These however, were not the first articulated cars in the United States as a firm in Cleveland, Ohio, named Brewer and Krehbiel built a complete unit which went into service on July 24th, 1893.

Trailers were rarely seen in Britain after steam traction disappeared from the tramways. The Liverpool system, electrified in 1898, started with 18-seat trailers hauled by small 20-seat motorcars built in Hamburg. Trailers also ran for a short time behind electric cars in Bristol, Coventry and Grimsby in the early days of electric traction and one combination worked in Birmingham during the 1914-18 war, but the longest and largest experiment with them was in London from 1913 to 1924. To begin with, eight old horse cars were used as trailers and when 150 new trailers were bought they were constructed in much the same style with open-top bodies on four-wheel trucks. These combinations were confined to four southern routes, as the Metropolitan Police resisted their introduction north of the Thames. It was the police, too, who had stopped an experiment between Euston and Hampstead with coupled single-deckers

in 1911. The trailers were useful during the war as they saved manpower but they were a hindrance to really fast working.

The problem of how to serve roads which obviously needed transport, but where the high cost of permanent way construction daunted even the most optimistic, was early in the minds of tramway engineers. Dr Werner von Siemens, already referred to in connection with early developments in Germany, designed a railless electric vehicle drawing current from overhead wires as early as 1881 and it ran in Berlin for a time the following year. Then there was an interval of some years, but from 1899 development of the trackless or railless tram was continuous. It will make things easier for the reader if the rise of this hybrid is dealt with in the next chapter, when we shall discuss the first clear indications that the electric tramway era was to be a short one.

The 1914-18 war produced little material damage to undertakings in Britain through enemy action, but as the war went on both bus and tram systems suffered greatly from shortage of staff and lack of repair facilities. The London General temporarily lost 1,600 buses of which 1,300 went overseas, and it took many months for the company to recover after hostilities

ended. In May, 1919 the General could only put 2,044 buses on the road for daily services as against 2,906 in 1914. The tram situation was as bad or worse. At the same date the L.C.C. owned 1,662 cars (it had sold 59 to help other systems) and 158 trailers and could only turn out for service 1,210 and 112, compared with 1,452 and 158 when war broke out.

The drain on manpower can hardly be realized today and things were made particularly difficult for managements by the rush to volunteer in the early days of the war. Provincial undertakings were as badly hit as London, worse perhaps. The Glasgow trams, with a normal staff of about 6,000, lost over 3,000 men to the services before 1918. Women had to be brought in and in Glasgow they not only conducted but 33 of them drove trams, too.

Nearly all petrol omnibuses in the provinces were commandeered and those few undertakings who had gone in for petrol-electric machines were fortunate in that the Army did not want them. Some tried to make do with battery electrics, while coal-gas carried in large balloons on the roof enabled a service to be given in other places.

In Belgium and Northern France destruction was

terrific and, where light railways or tramways did not actually suffer from the fighting, their installations were often robbed by the Germans to keep their own systems going. Thus of the 4,095 km. of vicinal lines working in Belgium in 1914 only 1,865 were still intact at the end of the war.

America, of course, escaped material damage but it was during the war years that a portent of things to come appeared. New York had had buses on Fifth Avenue from 1905 but they were regarded as an isolated freak. In the summer of 1914 someone driving a T-model Ford in Los Angeles started pulling up at car stops and offering rides at a 'jitney' (5 cents) a head. Within six months Los Angeles had 700 or so of these 'pirates' and soon every urban street railway in the country was menaced by them. But the street-car companies fought back and, under pressure of legislation and the rising costs occasioned by the war in Europe into which the U.S. entered in 1917, most jitney owners were eventually forced out of business. Those who survived became owners of orthodox buses. In 1916 interurban electric mileage reached its peak and every year thereafter more mileage was abandoned than was built.

The Roaring 'Twenties

In Britain the politicians promised that 'the war to end war' would lead to 'a land fit for heroes to live in'. The millions demobilized from the forces or discharged from the factories were soon disillusioned on that point, but the gratuities which the fighting men received were in many cases used to set them up in business and one business that attracted more men than any other was transport. Thousands of unwanted army vehicles were sold at almost give-away prices, particularly from a vast dump where the Slough Trading Estate is now.

There was no licensing control for goods vehicles at all and only in the major towns for passenger vehicles, so that the newcomers had virtually a free field. At first good profits were made but before long intense competition on the main roads forced hundreds of men out of business with the loss of their capital. Nevertheless many did survive, particularly in country districts and many a present-day bus route dates from 1919-20. The ex-army vehicles were, of course, basically goods carriers and in the early post-war years chassis were used indiscriminately, very often with a lorry body on weekdays and some rough seats fixed up for the weekends.

London, too, saw lorry-buses. There was such a shortage of vehicles in the spring of 1919 that the General fixed up a hundred or so lorries with rear steps, seats and tilts (canvas roof-covers) as a temporary measure. With remarkable speed it produced by August of the same year a completely new design, the 'K' type with 46 (instead of 34) seats. With its straight sides instead of the old curved rocker panel it provided transverse seating on the lower deck and, with the driver positioned partly on top of the engine, a longer body space was available.

In London the police until 1930 could exercise a veto on the design of buses and trams and their conservatism put London well behind many other towns in constructional details. Top covers on buses, wider bodies, pneumatic tyres and windscreens all came to London long after they were accepted elsewhere. Each improved type meant a fresh fight with the police.

The classic example of this obstructionism was the trouble with the 'NS' type. First built in 1923, this had a single-step platform and was specially constructed with a low centre of gravity so that the top could be roofed over. More than once both in horse and motor days buses had appeared with awnings experimentally arranged over the top deck but completely covered-in

buses were suspect on safety grounds, despite the
fact that four operated quite successfully in Widnes,
Lancashire, from 1909 until the top-covers were
taken off so that gasbags could be fitted as a wartime
economy measure.

The Metropolitan Police would not agree to the
'NS' being covered in until the autumn of 1925 and
although single-deckers began to appear on pneumatic
tyres in the same year (at least two years after they
became commonplace in the provinces), it was not
until 1928 that they were permitted on the 'NS'.

The General's virtual monopoly was rudely shaken
on August 5th, 1922, when A. G. Partridge, D. F.
Jermyn and A. S. Griffin put a bus on the famous
route 11 (Liverpool Street – Shepherds Bush) with
the fleet name Express. At that time although the
Metropolitan Police had such absolute powers over
the constructional details of vehicles, neither they nor
anyone else had power to define routes or fares. The
first Express was on a Leyland chassis with Dodson
46-seat body. Partridge, Jermyn and Griffin were
copied by dozens of others who saw that there was
money to be made in the demand for better transport
in London. Eventually there were some 680 independent buses running on the London streets.

The General was hard-pressed, but the trams were
in an even worse plight. Not only had their vehicles
suffered through lack of maintenance during the war
but many miles of track needed relaying. This expensive job now had to be undertaken largely for the
benefit of other users. Hordes of motor lorries and,
more ironically, of competitive motorbuses descended
on the main roads on which the bulk of tramway
revenue was earned.

Although at the end of the 1920s there was considerable deflation accompanied by widespread de-
creases in wages, in the earlier years of the decade
prices rose high over 1914 figures. The tram-men, by
securing a reduction in hours from 54 to 48, obtained
in effect a rise in wages, but this was insufficient. In
1924 after the employers, because of the financial
situation, had rejected a request for a rise of eight
shillings a week, all the London tramway men struck
and the staffs of the General and its associates stopped
work in support. (Strikes were exceptionally rare on
British tramway systems before 1939, because for one
thing they offered a security of employment that few
other workers had.)

An immediate result of the strike was the passing
of the London Traffic Act, 1924, which compelled

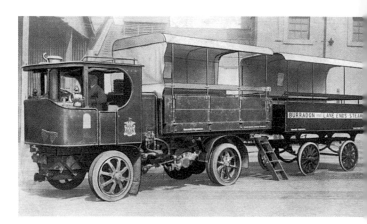

operators to work to published route- and time-tables and restricted the number of buses to be operated on all main roads, except on Sundays.

The competition also had the effect of urging the tramway undertakings to effect service and stock improvements. The London County Council appeared to the casual observer to be extremely conservative. The 125 new cars delivered in 1920 looked outwardly very little different from the class 'E' cars which first appeared in 1906, but in fact the council was continually making modifications so that in 1914 it had a highly efficient fleet. In particular the use of the magnetic track brake as the service brake enabled the council's cars to achieve a much higher average speed than those of any other municipal undertaking in the country.

The L.C.C. also fought the competition with cheap fares. In 1912-3 it had introduced a maximum of 3d. single (5d. return) anywhere in the county, the longest ride possible for this low figure being the journey of over 13 miles from Victoria Embankment to Abbey Wood. Transfers where no direct service was provided were an early feature of the council's operations and this facility was greatly increased when in 1920 cheap midday fares (available roughly from 10 a.m. to 4 p.m.) were introduced. The midday maximum then became only 2d. with three stages (instead of two) for 1d. Then in 1925 came the shilling all-day ticket giving unlimited rides in the county for 24 hours. This was extended in the late '20s to include the east London municipal systems (except Ilford) and also Croydon. The buses never attempted to compete with the all-day ticket but they had to give cheap midday fares on common sections of routes.

The new trams which the L.C.C. ordered in the second half of the decade (including some powerful four-motored cars for hilly routes) marked a great advance in speed and comfort. The tramway com-

panies after a number of experiments produced the Feltham class of which 100 were built. These great vehicles were designed to give a high degree of comfort in the slack hours with ample standing room in the peaks. Those municipalities which had inter-running arrangements with the L.C.C. also improved their stock

It was clear, however, that some greater degree of co-ordination was necessary for Londoners to have the very best possible service. This was no new idea. But for a change of political control, it could have come about in 1906 when the Underground was in such low water that if the L.C.C. had advanced £5 million at 4 per cent it could have had the right to purchase in twenty-one or forty years. Then in 1913 there were negotiations between the County Council and the combine which were to have been the subject of a parliamentary bill in November, 1914. The war killed this. Further negotiations in 1915 were unsuccessful. There was another attempt to organize a pool of receipts and unified management in 1928-9 which nearly succeeded, but again politics intervened and the negotiations fizzled out.

The impact of the motorbus on other British tramway systems was rather different. Most town systems were municipally owned and protected to some extent by the corporations having licensing powers, so that private buses were prevented from plying within the municipal boundaries. There was no means however, of stopping buses from outside bringing in passengers at return fares and it was soon found that people living near the boundaries took advantage of this and forsook the trams.

Where undertakings such as Glasgow and Leeds ran well outside their own boundaries they found that great inroads were being made into their receipts from the out-boundary services. Glasgow in particular was hit badly but the corporation responded with

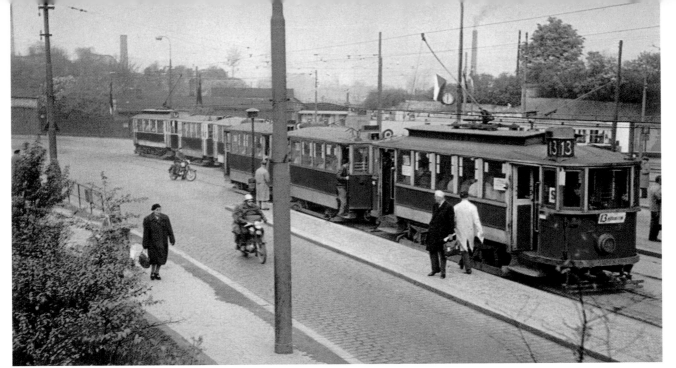

great vigour. It not only speeded up its cars and built new and faster ones but introduced fares which even beat London's for cheapness.

In Bristol the corporation took care to protect the company-operated trams and the tramway company developed such extensive country services itself (and also built its own vehicles) that it was able to maintain its finances very well.

It was an entirely different story in Stoke-on-Trent, where the council stupidly licensed any bus owner who chose to apply. The fantastic result was that at one time there were 70 operators in the city, most of them working on the 11-mile main tram route. Owing to the uncertainty of future municipal policy the tramway company had not modernized its undertaking and the trams, with their single-track lay-out, were hopelessly beaten. The Potteries Electric Traction Co. had to scrap them, write off £355,226 and turn over completely to buses.

Competition ran wild even in Ireland but both the Belfast Corporation and the Dublin United Tramways Co. survived and improved their tram services. The Dublin company had a particularly difficult time during 'the troubles' when trams made useful barricades during street fighting.

One important feature of the '20s in Britain was the emergence of the 'area agreement companies'. The British Electric Traction group had well-established spheres of influence through its tramway undertakings, so had the National Electric Construction Co. and the Balfour, Beatty group. Among the concerns with pre-1914 origins which pushed out into the provinces were the National, after it gave up steam operation, and the very old firm of Thomas Tilling.

A more recent power in the land was United Automobile Services which started at Lowestoft in 1912 and soon after in Durham and spread thence into several counties. There was a joint group, Tilling-B.E.T., comprising companies in which both Tilling and B.E.T. had shares. By 1929 most of the major bus companies in England and Wales were in one of these five groups, in all of which one or other of the main line railways acquired an interest.

Some enterprising municipalities also staked out spheres of influence well beyond their boundaries and although some subsequently withdrew, Sheffield, Walsall and Wolverhampton still operate long country routes.

This, too, was the age of the 'sharra'. A char-à-bancs was, as its name implies, originally drawn

Left: Modern tram car in the centre of Copenhagen
Below left: A car with pantograph in Stockholm
Below: Trams drawn up in the Karlsplatz in Munich

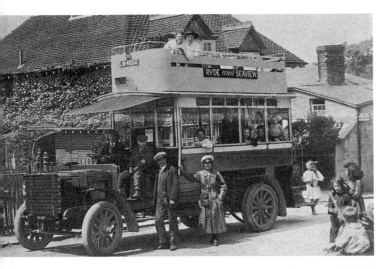

Left: The last steam bus in service in Britain, at Ryde in 1923

Centre: Barton's of Nottingham equipped this bus with a marine engine in 1929

Below: What happened when the London General tried to design a tram for the London United; 'Poppy' passing Chiswick Works, where it was built in 1928

by horse and had cross-bench seating. The motor pioneers of the '20s soon began to offer seaside and country pleasure rides and when vehicles were used which were a little more luxurious than the lorry-cum-bus they were called chars-à-bancs, which became anglicized to 'sharrabang' and so to 'sharra'.

There had been some long-distance touring before 1914 but this was an adventure indeed! It was hard going even in the early '20s when solid tyres were the rule, but by the end of the decade 'coaching' was commonplace and a network of long-distance services had sprung up.

The Potteries trams were not the first to go. Apart from short branch lines here and there and some horse lines which were never converted, Sheerness was the first system to be abandoned; this was in 1917. True it was only a tiny undertaking and so were Neath (with its gas trams) and Taunton, scrapped in 1920 and 1921 respectively, but from 1924 onwards the pace increased. It was in that year that Keighley changed over to trolleybuses and this is an opportune moment to refer further to these hybrid vehicles.

Dr Werner von Siemens, to whom the electrical industry owes so much, conducted early experiments with railless vehicles drawing current from overhead

wires. A notable vehicle was demonstrated in Berlin
in 1899 which could run either on or off rails. At the
Paris Exhibition of 1900 a trolleybus operated for a
few months to connect the exhibition with the Porte
de Vincennes. There were other experiments in Germany, France, Austria and Italy and in 1908 the
Railless Electric Traction Co. was formed in England.

At first systems employing small four-wheeled
trolleys (or 'trollers') running on the twin overhead
wires were favoured, but gradually the idea of rigid
swivelling trolleypoles gained ground. On some early
installations a single pole with double head was used
and this type lasted at Drammen in Norway until the
1960s. In Britain twin poles were advocated by the
Railless Electric Traction Co., whose early vehicles
were fitted with two motors as in tramcars and also
with tram-type controllers.

The first 'trackless trams' put into service in Great
Britain were at Leeds and Bradford. Both systems were
formally opened on June 20th, 1911, but the public
was not admitted to the Bradford route until the 24th.
The original Leeds route was along Whitehall Road
into the city centre while the Bradford one linked
suburbs on the eastern periphery. Leeds subsequently
opened two other short routes in prolongation of the

Yeadon tram route but gave up trolleybus operation in 1928. At Rotherham in 1912 trolleybuses were introduced between Wickersley and Maltby instead of extending the tram service; this line lasted until 1954.

Leeds was not the first place to abandon the 'track-less'. At Dundee two railless cars so cut up the road surface that they only lasted less than two years from starting in September, 1912. An experiment in the Rhondda Valley in South Wales was equally short-lived and four very short routes in Aberdare were only worked from 1913 to 1925. Stockport had a single route from 1913 to 1919. Halifax and Oldham were other places which gave up before Leeds did, but Keighley was particularly interesting.

In 1913 the Cédès-Stoll system (which was one of those employing a 'troller' running on the overhead) was adopted on three roads as extensions of existing tram routes, but difficulties during the 1914-18 war caused the gradual replacement of the Cédès-Stoll vehicles by motorbuses. Then in 1924 Keighley abandoned its small tram system altogether and introduced a second trolleybus system, this time using the more normal collection by trolley booms. This, too, had only a fairly short life, until 1932.

The small Lancashire town of Ramsbottom was the

first place in Britain to start a trolleybus service where there had never been trams. In fact the only other example of this is the Tees-side Railless Traction Board which still runs trolleybuses, whereas Ramsbottom gave up before 1930.

It was largely thanks to Tees-side that trolleybuses really got going in Britain. Instead of using vehicles which were conceived as trackless trams, J. Boothroyd Parker the manager there in 1922, took a Tilling-Stevens petrol-electric bus and adapted it to run either as a trolleybus or a motorbus.

Ipswich changed over to trolleybuses in 1923-7 and Darlington in 1926 and for the next quarter of a century both managed without any motorbuses at all, the trolleybus system becoming considerably more extensive than the tram system.

The biggest change-overs to trolleybuses before 1930 were at Wolverhampton and Hastings, both interesting systems which at one time had had alternatives to the overhead system of current collection. Wolverhampton operated its trams successfully on the surface-contact (or stud) system for many years while along the front at Hastings, to avoid the 'unsightly' overhead, cars were first operated by another form of surface-contact system and then from 1914 to 1921

Left: Standard Paris bus of the 1920s at Porte St Martin

Below, far left: Daimler-Benz 60-seat double-decker of 1926

Below left: Motrice L, the standard Paris car after 1924

In colour: A Glasgow single-deck trolleybus

by petrol engines generating current for the traction motors. Wolverhampton became world-famous through the successful design and operation of trolleybuses by C. Owen Silvers, its manager for many years.

As the '20s advanced the pace of tramway replacement by either motor or trolleybus increased but in 1930 it still seemed as if the streetcar must remain predominant for mass movement.

Meanwhile in France all the buses and trams in the Seine Département and parts of Seine-et-Oise were taken over by the local authority in 1921-4 and put under the management of La Société des Transports en Commun de la Région Parisienne. The *départements* provided the capital for the purchase of the former companies and the reconstruction of the permanent way and equipment where necessary with new rolling stock, leaving the S.T.C.R.P. to function thereafter as a commercial enterprise.

The new concern had not only to deal with wartime arrears of maintenance but to standardize an enormous variety of rolling-stock. It took over some 50 different types of motorcar and about 40 different types of trailers stored in 34 depots. In all about 2900 cars and trailers were involved, and 734 motorbuses.

In reorganizing and replacing much of this heterogeneous fleet the last of the double-deck streetcars were scrapped except for a few retained as trailers on the rural steam-operated roadside line to Arpajon. A notable improvement was the introduction of control-trailers so that the need for turning circles was obviated on some routes. On others multiple-unit operation enabled rakes of four vehicles to be operated without loss of speed.

The Paris tramway system reached its maximum in 1925 when 114 routes were operated over some 440 street miles (700 km.). The bus fleet which the S.T.C.R.P. took over was growing throughout the '20s also.

At this time the local authorities in the Paris area were planning a vast scheme for radial motorways extending in all directions from a new ring road right round the capital. The S.T.C.R.P. planned to join in this by constructing tramway reservations along all the radials with proper interchange at the ring road junctions. In some cases tracks were to have been duplicated to enable expresses to run. Had construction been undertaken at the time, the new facilities could have been completed before the suburbs built up but financial stringency killed the scheme.

Left: Cédès-Stoll trolleybus being demonstrated at West Ham in 1912

Below: Another early trolleybus at Farnley Moor Top, Leeds

Bottom left: The first trolleybus in Ipswich, 1923

Bottom right: A new Leyland Titan squeezing under the Stonebow in Lincoln, 1927

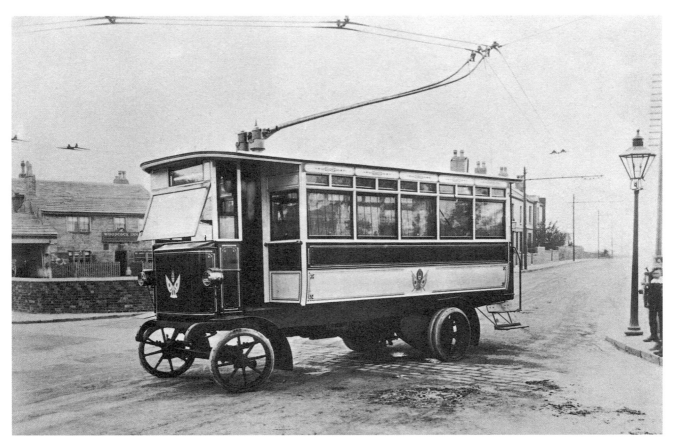

Below: The Keystone Cops get their motor crushed between a pair of unyielding streetcars

Right: A Hupmobile of 1919, from which sprang the vast Greyhound empire in the U.S.A.

Centre right: Buses for charter lined up by the roadside in Brooklyn, 1924

Bottom right: Indiana car crossing a country highway at speed

When the war ended in 1918 Berlin and its suburbs were being served by seven large and several smaller tram systems as well as the Hochbahn (the 'elevated' but, in fact, largely underground railway) and ABOAG. All the boroughs in Greater Berlin were merged into one local authority in 1920 and this in 1920-1 took over all the tram systems adding the Hochbahn in 1927 and ABOAG in 1929, thus creating the Berliner Verkehrs Gesellschaft (B.V.G.). The Berlin undertaking's greatest trouble was inflation, which led to the financial collapse of 1923 and the drastic closure of many routes. In the difficult circumstances of the time there was a very creditable revival in the late '20s, when Berlin had the largest tram fleet under one control in the world.

In Vienna, too, the transport undertaking not only survived the financial crises of the '20s but improved its services, too. An interesting move was the incorporation into the municipal system of a circular steam-operated railway round the inner city (something like the Paris 'Petite Ceinture'), its connection to the tramway network and conversion to electrical working, which came into effect in 1925.

A great many American street railways never recovered from the arrears of maintenance that piled up at the end of the war and fell an easy prey to the growing number of buses that appeared on rural and suburban routes. As new lines were built their mileage was more than counterbalanced by abandonments. After 1923 the total of passengers carried, after rising steadily for decades, began to fall continuously. At first most trolley lines refused to consider the bus seriously. It is said that in 1920 all the trolley lines in the U.S.A. owned in total less than 75 buses! But, within a very few years, buses became a recognized feature of rural life and in 1925 there were estimated to be some 6,500 operators in the States, each, however, only owning an average of two buses. This was about the date that consolidation really began. The Motor Transit Corporation, at first operating between Muskegon, Grand Rapids and Chicago was formed in 1926 and expanded rapidly, mainly east of Chicago.

Other names which became prominent about this time were of two old-established concerns, Pickwick Stage Lines of Los Angeles, dating from 1910 and Pioneer Yelloway System which had developed from the days of the horse stage and by this time was working trans-continental coaches. In 1929 these two concerns amalgamated with the bus section of the South-

ern Pacific Railroad to form Pacific Greyhound Lines. Between California and the Mississippi the Pickwick and Pioneer routes were combined as Pickwick-Greyhound Lines. The urge to this consolidation was the purchase of Pioneer by the Motor Transit Corporation, which was proceeding at the same time to acquire other existing businesses (or a share in them) so rapidly that by 1930 nearly every state in the Union was served by coaches with the fleet name, Greyhound.

It was not only in North America that the jitney menaced the streetcar. One of the biggest tramway undertakings in the world was that of the largely British-owned Anglo-Argentine Tramways Co. in Buenos Aires. Throughout the 1920s this was attacked by *collectivos*, originally large private cars and later what are now called minibuses. Not only did Anglo-Argentine have to compete with these but the government refused it permission to raise its fares to counter post-war inflation. It became a victim of local politics and the eventual loss to the British stockholders was tremendous. In Australia the creation of the Melbourne and Metropolitan Tramways Board signalled the beginning of the end for the extensive cable system in the capital of Victoria.

THE TROUBLED 'THIRTIES

The great slump which started in the United States and spread all over the western world from 1929 onwards had a marked effect on road transport and in particular accelerated the changeover from electric traction to motor bus. Worst hit were the American interurbans. A significant decline began in 1925 and each year thereafter more mileage was abandoned.

In the nine years, 1925-33, 7,852 route miles were abandoned and, although the pace thereafter declined as business in general picked up, there were only some 2,700 miles left in September, 1939, compared with the peak figure of 15,580 miles in passenger service in 1916. These figures do not include the rural trolley lines in New England all of which went by the early 'thirties.

Most of the Pacific Electric system was still in operation when war came and there was a considerable mileage around Chicago, St Louis and Pittsburgh and in Illinois and Iowa, but elsewhere only an odd line or two survived, mainly as a freight carrier.

Dramatic as was the decline of the interurbans, the city street railways did not give in so quickly. In 1929, twenty-five of the largest companies formed the Electric Railway Presidents' Conference Committee and allocated a million dollars for a team to design the

ideal car. The result after five years was the famous P.C.C. car, which in smooth acceleration and braking, high intermediate speed and passenger comfort on good welded tracks made the competitive buses of the day back numbers. Most appropriately, this ultimate in streetcar design was available in time for Frank Sprague to ride in it a few weeks before he died. But it was a dozen years too late. With another world war approaching few concerns were prepared to risk the large capital sums needed to re-equip completely the remaining urban systems. In all only about 1,100 P.C.C. cars were built before 1939, but if the work put into the project failed to save the American streetcar industry it had a lasting effect elsewhere.

Not, it is often regretted, in the British Isles where the situation was complicated by the tendency for towns to sprawl rather than to build upward, by the ring fence erected round many municipal undertakings which often prevented effective co-ordination, by the British devotion to double-deckers and, perhaps more than all these by the enthusiastic acceptance in

Above: Broadgate, hub of the Coventry transport system, in 1938; for a before-and-after contrast in city planning, see the view of the new Broadgate on page 116.

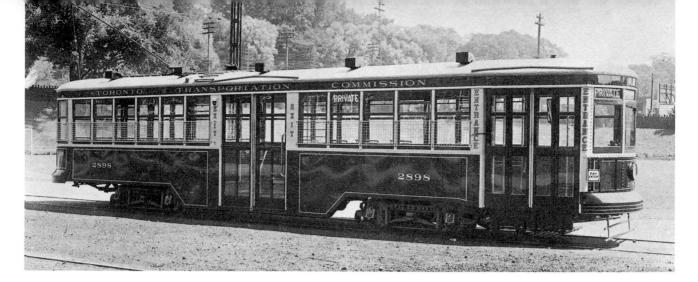

Britain of the compression-ignition engine and its rapid development before the Chancellor of the Exchequer realized it existed and decided to tax its fuel as punitively as he was taxing petrol.

The compression-ignition engine (or the diesel as it is now more usually called) dispenses with the ignition system and carburetter of the petrol engine, but on the other hand requires extremely precise fuel-measuring and injection equipment. Its great advantages are its economy in fuel and its high torque or pulling power at low speeds. Both these qualities are assets in countries where heavy traffic exists and there is no indigenous source of liquid fuel. In America where gasoline was cheap and abundant the economy of the diesel mattered much less.

In its early stages the substitution of diesel for petrol engines in commercial vehicles added so much to the unladen weight that many operators (having in mind the taxation scales then in force) thought twice before making a change. Curiously enough, it was a four-cylinder engine designed by Gardner

Bros. of Patricroft, Lancashire, for marine propulsion that showed how practical a diesel could be for bus work. This engine was fitted into a bus operated by Barton Bros. of Beeston, Nottinghamshire, a family firm well-known for three generations for enterprise in both engineering and operation. The date was 1929. In the next year Sheffield Corporation started using a Karrier with a Benz engine and this example was followed by the corporations of Leeds and Manchester, who bought Crossleys with Gardner engines.

The practicability of the diesel offered another possible choice to the tramway operators who were wondering about the future. Ignoring those systems which were never electrified, by the end of 1930, 34 tramway undertakings in the British Isles had turned over to motorbus operation, all with petrol machines, and 11 to trolleybuses, supplemented in three cases by a few motorbuses. Except for the Potteries company, mentioned earlier, and Wolverhampton Corporation, none of the 45 was a very large undertaking, most of the fleets consisting of 40 or fewer cars.

It is interesting to note that of the 34 which changed directly to motorbuses only eight were municipalities while, on the other hand, only three of those who preferred 'trackless' were not and one of

Top: A Peter Witt-type car in Toronto, 1932

Above: America's fastest interurban, the Galveston-Houston line

Below: View of a tram driver's platform with removable hand controls used for driving either end of the car, handbrake staff, wheel for applying slipper brake and pedals for gong and sand supply

Right: The Presidents' Conference Committee car, the ultimate in American design of the '30s

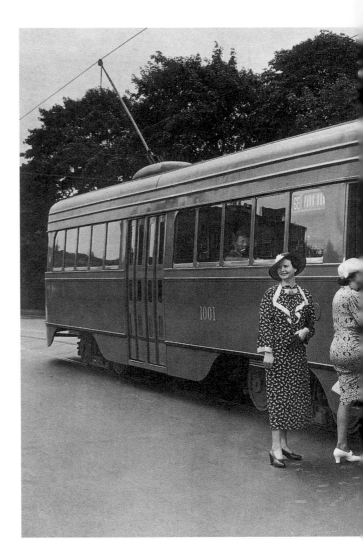

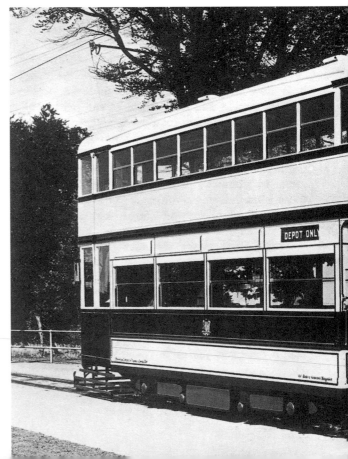

these, simultaneously with the conversion, sold its business to Wolverhampton Corporation. Most which converted had had a high proportion of single-track and a consequent slow service.

Many British electric tramways had grown out of a joint electricity supply and transport undertaking and where a concern continued to be the local provider of light and power there was a strong argument for continuing to make use of the generating plant. The attitude to trolleybuses in the 1930s was thus different from what it was in earlier years. Before 1914 they were thought of as extensions to tram routes where the cost of laying a permanent way would not be justified in the first instance. After 1918, they began to be thought of as possible substitutes, especially when pneumatic tyres for heavy vehicles became possible.

There were two other factors to be considered also in Great Britain. The Road Traffic Act, 1930, instituted a licensing system which took away from bus operators much of the freedom they had previously enjoyed. No longer could a council or company juggle its fares as it thought fit or put on a bus here or there. The newly appointed traffic commissioners had the last word, but they had no control over trams or trolleybuses.

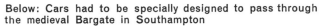

Below: Cars had to be specially designed to pass through the medieval Bargate in Southampton

Below left: The last tram built for service in Birmingham, 1930

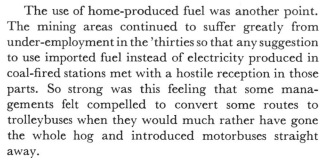

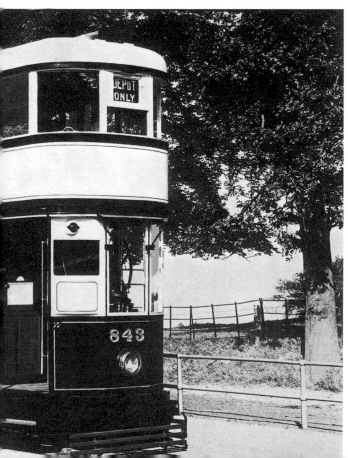

The use of home-produced fuel was another point. The mining areas continued to suffer greatly from under-employment in the 'thirties so that any suggestion to use imported fuel instead of electricity produced in coal-fired stations met with a hostile reception in those parts. So strong was this feeling that some managements felt compelled to convert some routes to trolleybuses when they would much rather have gone the whole hog and introduced motorbuses straight away.

Manchester is the classic case of this. The corporation had a large tram fleet of over 900 cars at its maximum and interworking arrangements with surrounding local authorities. Nearly all its mileage was double-tracked but for some unexplained reason it had never attempted really fast operation until 1929. Up to that time cars had to be pulled up by the hand-brake, whereas in almost every other large system air or magnetic-track brakes were used. Some new air-braked cars were ordered in 1929, but just at this time a route (no. 53) which formed three-quarters of a circle round the city needed renewal. Stretches of single track had made speeds even slower than was general in Manchester and low railway bridges prevented the use of double-deckers.

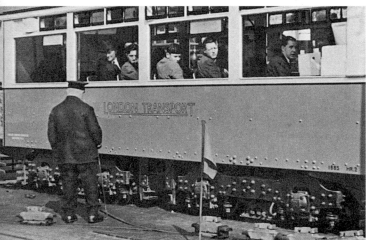

Two years before this, Leyland Motors had introduced the low-bridge 'Titan' which by the use of a sunken gangway on the offside of the upper deck made it possible to reduce the height of a double-decker from about 14ft. 6in. to less than 13ft. The design has never been a popular one with either the travelling public or the conductors, but hundreds of such buses have been built and double-deck services have been possible which could not otherwise have run.

The new low-bridge double-decker was tried on service 53. The 54-minute tram journey was reduced to 43 minutes and passengers increased in a year by 11 per cent, despite the beginning of the depression. Yet when Manchester decided eventually that all its trams must go, a number of routes on the east and north-east sides of the city were converted to trolleybus operation, although these were not the routes of densest traffic and several involved interworking arrangements with other operators.

On the other side of Lancashire, quite a different view was taken. Liverpool Corporation bought out a local bus company in 1911 and ordered a few new vehicles in the 1920s but for many years after, no municipal motorbus was to be seen on any main

Right: At the reopening ceremony of the Kingsway Subway in London, 1931

Below: One of the first trolleybuses in London, introduced by the London United Tramways Co., 1931

route. From 1914 each of many new extensions to the tramways was laid on reserved track and this method of segregating tram traffic was adopted on some of the older sections. Because of wartime needs Liverpool's tramway mileage continued to grow until the late date of 1943 by which time nearly 28 route miles was on reservation.

But this is running ahead. In 1932 it was decided to retain and modernize the tramways and from 1935 onwards some remarkably fine cars were produced, 313 of them in all, including the famous eight-wheeled 'Green Goddesses'.

Sunderland was another undertaking which also modernized in the 'thirties. Sheffield and Leeds retained their faith in the tram and Glasgow built, in 1938, some of the finest vehicles which have ever run on street tracks. Edinburgh produced some fast light-weight cars and Blackpool had several new types. Birmingham dithered for several years. It began trolleybus operation on one route while still extending its trams. It converted another to motorbuses (petrol-driven), a third to trolleybuses and then decided to change the rest to diesel, despite the existence of long lengths of reserved track and a very heavy passenger traffic.

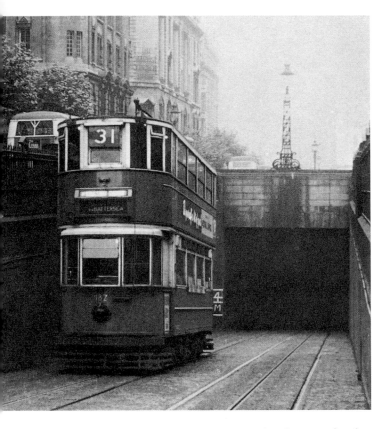

Between 1930 and the outbreak of war, 26 other British undertakings converted wholly or in part to trolleybus operation but only two started to use trolleybuses for the first time after 1939. Cardiff started in 1942 and Glasgow in 1949. The biggest of all the conversions was in London.

As we have already mentioned, negotiations for a pooling scheme between the Underground group (including the London General) and the London County Council tramways were reopened in 1928; they seemed to be in a fair way to success when they encountered an unexpected snag in the doctrinaire attitude of the government then in power. Prompted by the London Labour Party and its forceful leader, Herbert Morrison, complete public ownership was put forward as the only solution. How to bring this about wasted several years in argument before the London Passenger Transport Board came into existence on July 1st, 1933.

The effect of the London Passenger Transport Act was to vest the ownership of the Underground and all the trams and buses operating roughly within 30 miles of Charing Cross in one body, the members of which were appointed by certain named trustees, supposedly to represent various interests. The financial provisions of the Act satisfied no one, particularly the municipalities, and the problem of how to give the Board (and its successors) commercial freedom combined with public accountability and the responsibilities of a public utility has baffled successive governments ever since.

The new Board became the owner of about 3,000 railway cars, 6,732 buses and coaches, 2,630 trams and 61 trolleybuses. The average speed of the trams in 1930-1 including stops was 9.56 m.p.h. against the buses' 9.43. The L.C.C., with an average service interval of 1.67 minutes, was the most intensely operated tram system in the world.

While negotiations with the Underground were going on the London County Council continued to extend and improve its tram system. The Kingsway Subway, linking the northern and southern systems, was reconstructed to take double-deck cars and reopened on January 15th, 1931; a connection was made in Epping Forest to enable through cars to run to Woodford and in the following year, on June 30th, 1932, the last new tramway in the London area was opened when a service was put on along Westhorne Avenue. Also in 1932 a 6d. evening ticket was introduced giving unlimited rides after 6 p.m. on any municipal

system north of the Thames (except Ilford) or any L.C.C. or Croydon route south of it.

But perhaps the highlight of the year was the appearance of a magnificent new car, painted blue and gold, instead of the familiar red, and luxuriously upholstered and boldly numbered 1—the first of a brand-new fleet. Alas! It was the last tram ever built for London.

Before the L.P.T.B. came into being, the Underground group had for some years been considering the future of its tramways. A scheme was worked out to put the long route to Uxbridge on to reserved track as far as possible and this was one of the reasons for ordering the fast Feltham type of car mentioned in the last chapter. There seemed little future, however, for much of the London United system and it was decided to try the experiment of converting the routes radiating from Kingston to trolleybus operation. The new vehicles started work on May 16th, 1931, and with faster operating schedules and greater comfort, produced gratifying financial returns.

It is hardly surprising that the group decided to convert other poor traffic routes and when in 1933, the powers at 55, Broadway had all London Transport under their control, it was not long before a decision

was reached to change over the struggling ex-municipal systems of Erith, Bexley and Dartford. At the same time the Board said that the tram was still unbeaten as a mass-carrier and, although no new cars were built, improvements were made to many old ones.

Then in 1936, it was decided to convert the whole of the tram services to trolleybus operation, with the exception of a few miles where it was thought that motorbuses would fit better into the existing pattern. Difficulty was experienced in some areas in finding suitable turning circles. In some cases routes had to be shortened, and lengthened in others. The subway was the biggest problem, because of its width— narrow for buses to pass safely, although adequate for trams— the winding single tunnels at the southern end, the awkward debouchment at the northern end and the island platforms at the two stations. A trolleybus, No. 1374, was specially designed to work through the subway but as will be recounted later, no wires were ever erected for its use.

Work on this great conversion scheme was nearly half complete when war broke out. A certain amount continued until June 8th, 1940, when the last tram ran in Barking Road. North of the Thames this left only three services (sharing a common route from

Islington Green) which were retained because they worked through the subway to south London.

One early result of the war was the suspension of the express Green Line coaches which had grown up in this decade to link suburbs on opposite sides of the metropolis and to provide fast transits to the centre. Throughout Great Britain, indeed, a fine network of express services was developed from 1925 onwards, the year in which the formation of London Coastal Coaches provided a focal point for long-distance working into London. Another important date was 1934 when several major companies pooled some of their long-distance workings as Associated Motorways, based on Cheltenham. Unfortunately, services of express buses across Manchester to and from outlying towns were stopped in 1931 by a misguided decision of the first traffic commissioners.

Increasing congestion in Paris caused so much agitation for the removal of the trams that they disappeared in a much shorter time than those of London. A small mileage of little importance was lost in 1926-8, and then from 1930, abandonment took place at ever increasing speed. The Grands Boulevards, the market area and other central streets were cleared by 1934. It was at first thought that the outer sub-

Below: In the knacker's yard, 1938; trams being stripped down and broken up for scrap

In colour: A single deck-tram in Heidelberg (top) built at the turn of the century, contrasts with a streamlined car in Vienna

urban lines, much of them on reservations, would remain but in 1932 the surprising decision was made to replace the cars between Porte de la Chapelle and Saint Denis, a very heavy traffic route where the tracks were segregated from the carriageway. From then on suburban abandonments occurred as fast as those in the central area.

On March 15th, 1937, line 123/124, which made a semi-circle across the southern side of the city between Porte de Saint Cloud and Porte de Vincennes, closed down. All that was left of the once vast S.T.C.R.P. network was a short route of about 5 km. far out to the east between Le Raincy and Montfermeil. That ended on August 14th, 1938, when a private company put on a bus service in its place. Appropriately enough the first electrified line of the Paris system was the last.

Although the S.T.C.R.P. thus ended tramway operation before the last war, three small undertakings not far from Paris survived until after it.

Versailles had a quite separate town system which had a chequered career from 1876 onward until it was electrified in 1896. Four kilometres beyond the northern S.T.C.R.P. terminus at Pierrefitte one came to the tiny Villiers-le-Bel tramway, only 3 km. long,

linking that village with the station at Gonesse. Further out to the south of the city was the town system of Fontainebleu.

The urge to scrap trams was not so great in other populous cities in Europe and indeed many of the smaller systems in Germany, for example, as well as the larger ones, were extended during the 1930s. As tension grew after Hitler's accession to power, it became German government policy to encourage electricity in preference to imported fuel and where electricity was not practicable (as for goods vehicles) encouragement was given to the development of self-contained units, to produce gas from coal or coke. These were made available to bus users as well. As war loomed nearer thought was given to the possibility of using the trams for freight purposes.

In Belgium the S.N.C.V. went ahead with its policy of eliminating steam operation and where electrification was not justified economically it converted to *automotrices* of which by 1937 it had 250 with another 100 on order. Originally these trams with internal combustion engines (first used in 1925) were petrol-driven but diesel fuel proved successful in 1934 and no more petrol units were bought after 1937.

WAR–AND NO PEACE

When it became obvious that war was only a matter of days away, public lighting was drastically reduced in all the countries which expected to be involved. The limitation in Britain was much more severe than in the 1914-18 war when street lamps were not even partly blacked out until more than half way through hostilities. Vehicle lighting, too, was reduced to such an extent in 1939 that bus and tram indicators were almost useless after dark. Outside town limits operation was difficult in the extreme.

In London all Green Line coaches were taken off and in the provinces there was a great pruning of services so that vehicles and staff could be diverted to the transport of munition workers and troops. In the early days, the evacuation of school children from large cities had to be handled as well.

In the British Isles 43 undertakings were still running trams in 1939. In two cases, where conversion arrangements were far advanced, the trams ceased after the war had started; this also applied to routes north of the Thames in London. Local circumstances made two other abandonments inevitable but otherwise it was the government's intention that trams should continue, at any rate until the end of the war, in order to save imported fuel. At Bolton, Bradford and Coventry, routes already abandoned, but where the tracks had not been taken up, were brought back into service.

The first eight or nine months of the war brought few sensational incidents and little material damage but by the end of that time lack of maintenance and shortage of spares began to make themselves felt.

Then came the German invasion of Denmark, Norway and the Low Countries, including the destruction of the heart of Rotterdam and its tram system, and the beginning of the blitz on Britain. A large book could be written about the deeds of the men and women who kept the transport services going—about the staff of the East Kent Road Car Co., who served the only part of England that was both bombed and shelled, of the Birmingham tram drivers along 'Bomb Alley' (Bristol Road leading to the Austin works), of the London crews who reported for early turns despite almost sleepless nights—and so on all round the country.

Hardly a day passed in the big centres without the need to improvise and the task of the manage-

Above: Coventry's first war casualty in Pool Meadow bus station, 1940

ments was onerous in the extreme. The connoisseurs among the travellers enjoyed some extraordinary routings, especially when the London tram tracks were hit. The conduit system did not prove such a handicap as was expected thanks to surprisingly rapid first-aid work, but without the motorbuses there were many days on which London would have been at a standstill.

Two major blows were the destruction of the Bristol and Coventry tramways. At Bristol conversion was well on the way in 1939; the remaining routes ceased when, first, Bedminster depot was destroyed and then the power house was knocked out. All but a short length of the Coventry system was working on November 14th, 1940. The next morning the damage was found to be so widespread that the trams never ran again.

The special difficulties in London made it necessary to borrow buses extensively from the provinces and 473 were thus used at various times in 1940-1. There were many other transfers, too, particularly from the east coast towns, whence most of the population

Above: One of the disasters London Transport were faced with in 1940

had moved and which were banned as holiday resorts. Southend trolleybuses, for instance, were lent to Bradford.

Fuel supplies were an ever-present worry and it was hoped that producer gas might be a solution, so all commercial users were ordered to convert ten per cent of their fleets as a minimum. Although some vehicles had built-in producers it was usual for bus work to haul a small trailer on which the producer was mounted. The scheme was of doubtful value. The modifications to engines and then the maintenance of the producers were expensive in man-hours and the buses so fitted had poor acceleration and hill-climbing powers. The engines themselves suffered from increased wear-and-tear at a time when economy was of a paramount importance.

Until the fall of France, vehicle production was not greatly affected but in 1941 the government stopped all work on new buses. Obviously the country needed transport so vehicles which were partly finished and for which the necessary parts could be obtained were 'unfrozen'.

Several British undertakings received vehicles originally intended for overseas. London Transport, for instance, was allocated 43 trolleybuses and

Two streamlined coaches in St Peter's, Rome (top) and
Innsbruck, typical of the armies of tourist coaches which ply
across Europe in the summer

Right: An Austrian post bus seen in 1966 and, from Italy,
an articulated coach in the Piazzale Roma, Venice

Birmingham some motorbuses intended for South Africa. These were wider than the maximum then permitted in Britain and their successful operation was a powerful argument in the successful post-war agitation for greater width to be permitted.

The Ministry of Transport was given the task of allocating such new buses as were built and it was not long before the public had to make do with 'utility' models which were austere indeed.

The Guy Arab, which became the first standard double-decker, has now disappeared from the British scene but a few of the single-deck 32-seat Bedfords of which over 2,000 were built still remain in country districts with modified seating. In fact, many rural operators regret that something similar is not now obtainable. Later, Daimler and Bristol austerity double-deckers were produced.

When the war ended all operators had to make decisions on future policy. If they had trams or trolleybuses should they retain and modernize them or replace them with another type of vehicle? If they already had buses what size should future vehicles be and what should be their internal lay-out and so on?

In 1939 London Transport had already started to employ the newly designed 'RT' type of double-decker, seating 56, built (like the majority of its buses) on A.E.C. chassis and this, with modifications, was destined to be the standard from 1945 to 1956.

It had been intended to convert the remaining trams (mainly in south London) to trolleybus working after the war, but in 1946 it was decided to change over to motorbuses. At that time there seemed to be no thought of displacing the large trolleybus fleet and in fact 77 new trolleybuses were put on the road in 1948 and another 50 in 1952.

A start on the tramway conversion was made in October, 1950 and the last London tram ran into New Cross depot in the early hours of July 6th, 1952.

Far left: London bus damaged in a raid in October, 1940

Below left: As a wartime economy, town gas was tried by Barton Bros. of Nottingham and (left) other companies experimented with gas producer units

Below: Manchester's last tram rides to the depot in 1949 and a group of Mancunians make their last farewells

Bottom: Tramway graveyard at Charlton, London in 1950

Not all the cars were scrapped immediately. The last ever built (L.C.C. No. 1) and the serviceable Felthams were bought by Leeds; some of the trucks went to Alexandria. When the Leeds system was eventually closed No. 1 came back to London and is now in the Clapham Museum, together with one of the Felthams.

There were 36 undertakings still running trams at the end of the war, these varying in size from the one-horse and ten electric cars of the Great Northern Railway of Ireland to 1,000 or more vehicles. After the London conversion was complete, only 13 were left and three more of these went before 1955. Among them was Sunderland, which had so firmly twenty-five years before turned against the mania for conversion, while Liverpool, where in the '30s the policy of modernization had been so successful, was in process of changing over, too. In other places the future was uncertain but there still seemed a possibility that Britain might enter the final years of the century with several large tramway systems at work.

Glasgow was a particularly bad case of indecision largely because of local and national politics. Over the years the corporation had provided a unified service, mainly by trams, over a wide radius from Glasgow Cross. It successfully resisted the attacks of the independents in the '20s and in the '30s put on the road some of the finest cars ever built. In 1945 there was no reason to suppose that electric traction would not remain supreme in Glasgow.

The city's power station was excepted when all other generating stations were nationalized and large sums were spent in 1948-9 on enlarging it. There were tram route extensions in 1949 and 100 new cars were ordered. So attached were the Glaswegians to their trams that, when it was proposed to convert a relatively lightly loaded route to trolleybus working, the proposal was so strongly contested that it was only carried in the full council by the Lord Provost's casting vote.

About this time an imaginative scheme was put forward by Mr E. R. L. Fitzpayne, the general manager of the undertaking, for utilizing the tramway reservations as light railways feeding into an underground steam-operated railway which would be converted to electrical working. A booklet issued by the corporation when the first trolleybus service started said, 'Trolleybuses, electrified trams and rapid transit electric cars are the obvious transport answers to the challenge of the new electric and atomic age'.

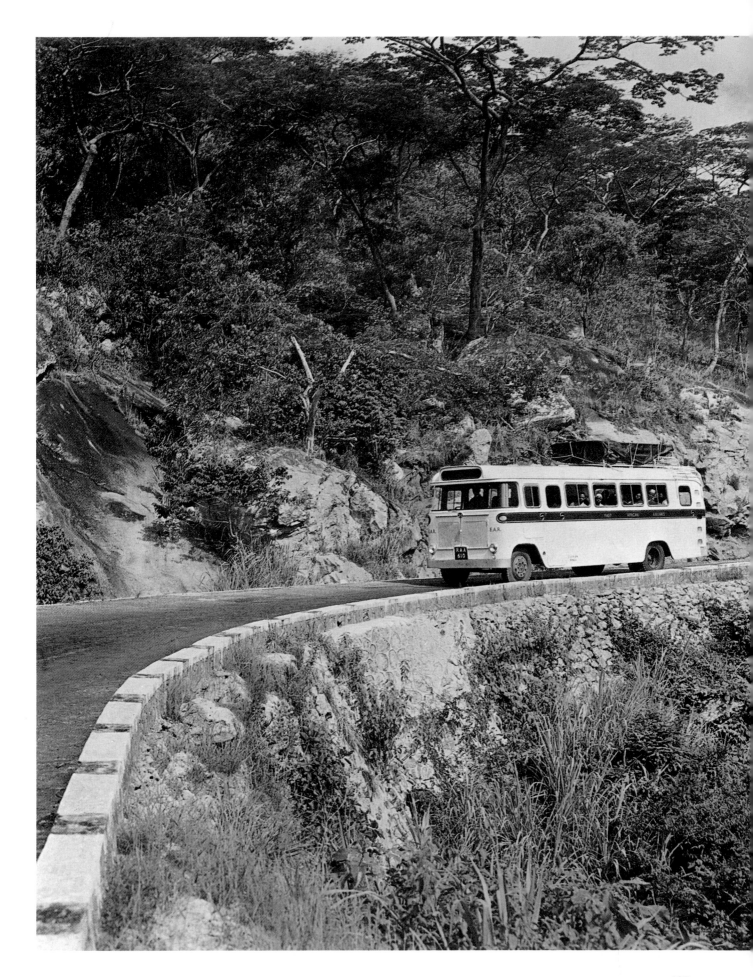

Below: Middleton tram in Boar Lane, Leeds

Right: Modern trolleybus at Old Steine, Brighton, 1959

Centre right: Feltham-type car originally designed for London but seen here in Leeds

Bottom: Promenade bus at Lytham, Lancashire, converted to open-top in 1950

Far right: Evening peak in Coventry, with 'Midland Red' and Corporation buses

But practice does not always mean the acceptance of the obvious and so it proved with Glasgow.

All British undertakings which had not been affected by evacuation had carried record numbers during the war and this state of affairs continued for several years because of the shortage of private cars and the fuel for them.

Then, about 1949-50, traffic began to decline. The recession was first noticed by operators of rural services and within two or three years many of them (usually owners of small businesses) found themselves in Queer Street. Misled by the post-war boom in demand for public transport, they had committed themselves heavily to hire-purchase for new vehicles and were now unable to keep up the payments. Services were drastically cut and many men went out of business.

Fares, which were still at 1939 level for the most part, were raised on both rural and urban services, as the slump very soon began to affect the revenues of town operators, too. Then the busmen got themselves into a vicious circle (or spiral) and this has continued ever since. The more they reduce services and/or raise fares the fewer passengers they carry and the harder it becomes to make the books balance.

One way in which it might be possible to break out of the spiral would be to carry more people at one time with fewer staff—in other words, by using larger buses without employing a conductor. On many rural services conductors had never been employed and there had been a number of experiments over the years on both electric trams and motorbuses to see if a conductor could be dispensed with, but the idea had never been favourably considered by the larger operators. The threatening circumstances caused a change of attitude but in many cases there was staff resistance.

It was fortunate for Paris that it had such an extensive system of underground railways as nearly all the 3,700 buses which it had in 1939 were out of service after the fall of France. Either they were seized by the Germans or the shortage of fuel and spare parts made them idle. Under the occupation the S.T.C.R.P. was merged with the Métro, which must have been even more crowded (if that is possible!) than it usually is.

When the Germans were defeated there were only three bus services running in central Paris and a few others operating from the outlying termini of the Métro. In November, 1945, six months after the liberation, there were still 1,273 motorbuses and six

trolleybuses unaccounted for. The inter-allied European Central Inland Transport Organization eventually traced most of these, scattered all over Europe, but some which got behind the Iron Curtain were never found.

By the end of 1947 the number of buses in service in the Paris area had only risen to 1,800, but from then onwards progress was steady, although it was clear that the ultimate size of the fleet would be less than in 1939. The usual pre-war bus was too small to be economic and it was decided to introduce larger vehicles, to be powered by diesel units instead of the engines fired by a mixture of commercial alcohol and low-grade petrol which the S.T.C.R.P. had favoured.

It has been mentioned that the Germans took six Paris trolleybuses. These must have been in almost new condition as the first trolleybus route in the city (apart from the early experiments), that from Champerret to Bezons, only started on January 18th, 1944. The vehicles used were similar to the then normal Paris bus with 28 seats and room for 24 standing. They were one-man-operated and carried a petrol-electric generator set for operation away from the wires.

In Belgium, although some rural services worked by autorails were changed to bus operation, many miles were electrified after the war and a new through route, 26 miles long, was opened from Charleroi to Namur. The standard-gauge system in Brussels was given new life by the formation of S.T.I.B. (la Société des Transports Intercommunaux de Bruxelles) half the company's capital being held by the State and local authorities and half by the shareholders of the old Tramways Bruxellois.

Visitors to Rotterdam at the end of the war were shown the entrance to an under-river tunnel with a single overhead wire. The Germans, having destroyed the centre of Rotterdam and the cross-river facilities, had thought of completing the Maas tunnel and running a trolleybus route through it, but somehow mishaps and breakdowns in the construction work occurred so frequently that they never finished the project.

Sabotage of this kind was brought to a fine art by the Dutch. The Germans took 300 trams and trailers for use in the Reich and they would have taken more had not defects occurred with remarkable frequency in those they earmarked just when it was planned to move them. In some cases the Dutch

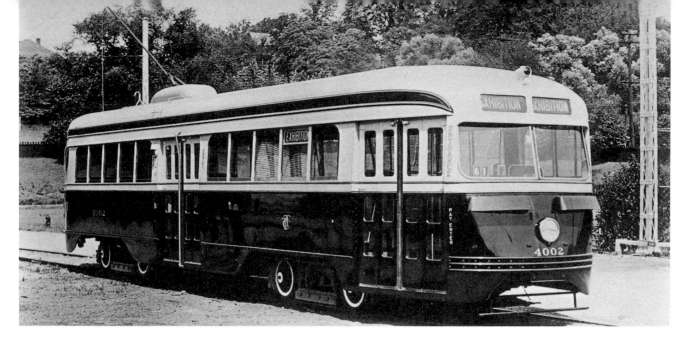

had difficulty in operating those trams they had left as supplies of overhead wire and other essentials ran out. The European Central Inland Transport Organization was able, as with the Paris buses, to recover most of the stolen trams but some were never returned from Russian-dominated territory.

In the immediate post-war years the most notable feature of the German scene was the absence of motor transport. The author travelled by road in May, 1946 from The Hague to Prague using different routes on the outward and homeward journeys and in the whole 1,445 miles only saw 13 buses east of Nijmegen. Some of the town tram systems, notably Würzburg and Bonn, were still out of action and no cars were running in the centre of Munich. The Frankfurt system, however, was working, although there were heaps of rubble alongside many of the tracks. Cologne, west of the river, was also functioning. On the whole the German tramways made a remarkably quick recovery, greatly helped by standardization of design for new cars.

In Berlin, goods services were maintained by tram for most of the war but by early 1945 most of the central tracks were useless through bombing and the electricity supply was only intermittent. A number

of burnt-out cars were filled with rubble and used as barricades against the invading Russian tanks. All public transport in the city had ceased when the war ended on May 8th, 1945.

One of the first duties of the Allied four-power control was to get some buses running while work started on restoring the tram system. Considerable progress was made in the first twelve months, but the pattern of services had to be radically altered, as much of the old centre had lost its importance. The introduction of a different currency in the American, British and French sectors in 1948 and the Russian blockade in 1948-9 started the train of events which eventually led to the permanent division of the undertaking into two parts.

Scandinavia did not abandon electric traction either in the immediate post-war years. Stockholm put into service some remarkably fine cars. A tram subway opened in 1933 was extended and plans were laid for the eventual conversion of the street tramways to light railways. Göteborg and Copenhagen also bought new cars and mention of Sweden recalls that it was a Swedish firm, Linjebuss, which in 1946 first began to organize a network of regular coach services throughout Western Europe.

The few American interurbans that were still carrying passengers in 1939 faded out during the war or in the decade or so after. Some town operations continued years after real interurban working had ceased. The largest of the interurban groups, the Pacific Electric Railway, which radiated from Los Angeles, had abandoned all except five routes by 1950 and these it sold in 1954 to Metropolitan Coach Lines, which quickly abandoned two of the routes. On the formation of the Los Angeles Metropolitan Transit Authority in 1957 it became owner of the remaining lines which were converted to bus operation in 1958-60.

A particularly interesting line was the Sacramento Northern which crossed the Sacramento River on a train ferry, ran over street tracks in Oakland and other towns and, from January, 1939, entered downtown San Francisco over the Bay Bridge. It abandoned passenger services in 1940-1.

Almost the last passenger-carrying interurban to go in the United States was the 14 miles Portland to Oregon City line of the Pacific Electric Power Co., which also had the longest life of any—65 years from 1893 to 1958. Most Canadian lines continued passenger services for a few years after the war but all

had given up by March, 1959 when the Niagara, St Catherine's and Toronto Railway's Thorold–Port Colborne service was abandoned.

It seemed as if three old-established interurban companies radiating from Chicago might go on for many years but today only the Chicago, South Shore and South Bend remains. New construction in 1956 enabled it to avoid street running in East Chicago and it now bears no resemblance at all to a street tramway.

The decline of the urban electric systems can be shown by a comparison of 1929 fleets and mileage with those of 1946. In the former year 56,980 street-cars and 57 trolleycoaches operated over 40,570 route miles; 17 years later the vehicle figures were 24,730 and 3,896 operating over 15,490 and 2,333 miles respectively. Buses owned by the operators whose fleets are included in these figures rose in the same period from 21,100 to 52,450.

Yet most of the city systems which were still working in 1945 had no plans for total abandonment. Much of the New York system was certainly run down and all cars had gone from Manhattan by 1949, but routes in the Bronx and in Brooklyn and Queen's were kept going. In many places there was talk of modernization and substantial orders were placed for P.C.C. cars. The Chicago Surface Lines had taken delivery of 200 of these by the end of 1947 and planned to have 600 in all. Philadelphia ordered 300 and St Louis 100; others went to Kansas, Washington, Boston, Minneapolis, Dallas and Detroit. By the summer of 1950 the 1,100 or so P.C.C.s in service in 1939 had grown to 4,872 in service or on order, and built to eight different gauges. Washington planned a seven-mile long subway for streetcars and intended systematically ordering new cars up to 1961.

Then there was an astonishingly rapid *volte face*. In 1950 Chicago still owned 2,329 streetcars, plus

Far left: Double-deck Daimler in Kowloon, Hong Kong

Left: The new way and the old, near Luxor in Egypt

Bottom left: Old open-sided tram in Cairo

Below: An unusual 'toastrack', closed on one side, at Douglas, Isle of Man

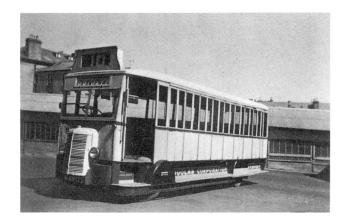

361 trolleycoaches and 1,050 motorbuses, but less than two years later, in September, 1952, the president of the Chicago Transit Authority announced that the street railway system would be reduced to three routes and that 400 of the 683 P.C.C.s would be converted for use on the elevated and subway rapid-transit routes. Several other undertakings changed their minds in a similar manner.

Toronto was consistent. It pinned its faith to electric traction, but decided to convert its most heavily loaded tramway, that along Yonge Street, into an underground railway. This was done and the Yonge Street Subway went into service in 1954.

One of the most notable features of American transport in the post-war decade was the definite establishment of the trans-continental bus, as an effective competitor with the railroads for long-distance traffic. The origins of the Greyhound business have been referred to in an earlier chapter. It survived the depression and within ten years of the war ending was providing services in every state of the Union and in Canada and over the Mexican border. In 1954 it put on the road the 1½-deck 40ft. long Scenicruiser, seating 43, and having twin diesel engines, air suspension, improved air-conditioning and toilet facilities. By 1957 it was operating some 7,000 vehicles. A similarly extensive service is provided by National Trailways, which is actually a joint-working organization of several operators.

The tram was not dead in Australia. It had 3,215 electric cars when 1949 opened. They were operating in five of the six state capitals (Perth had gone over to trolleybuses). Sydney had 1,398 and the following year ordered 250 more. Melbourne had 736 and was planning extensions, the most notable of which came to fruition in 1955 when the six-mile long Bourke Street route, once cable-operated, was changed from buses to trams.

FIGHTING FOR LIFE

In all the developed countries of the world operators of local passenger services have spent the last decade struggling to live against the competition of the private car. Rural areas have been deprived of hundreds of miles of routes, some old-established, because they no longer pay even bare running costs. In cities there has been the added problem of traffic congestion which has reduced vehicle availability and increased the cost of operation.

These circumstances alone would have made the fate of many undertakings uncertain, but, in some instances, the situation has been worsened by politics. Glasgow is a particularly clear example of this. In 1951 a government committee under the chairmanship of the late Sir R. Inglis recommended that Glasgow should give up its out-boundary services and scrap all its trams, while at the same time the state-owned railways should be electrified.

From then on, Glasgow was under continuous pressure to accept the report, although it meant breaking up a unified system and depriving the corporation of some good paying routes which were handed over to the state-owned bus companies and others. The Fitzpayne scheme, mentioned in the previous chapter, was quietly thrown into the waste-paper basket. The 100 new cars put into service in 1950-2 were followed by six more in 1954 and by 46 bought second-hand from Liverpool, but the corporation withdrew from Airdrie and Coatbridge in the east and Milngavie to the north-west in 1956 and from Paisley and Renfrew in the south-west the following year. Then, under pressure from one of the political parties, more tram routes were abandoned, ostensibly to get rid of 450 ancient cars. Some were converted to motorbus and some to trolleybus operation.

Glasgow has tried both double- and single-deck trolleybuses including some interesting single-deckers 35 feet long, for which special Ministry of Transport dispensation had to be obtained. The early enthusiasm for trolleybuses soon waned in face of the clamour for oil-engined buses from the predominant party on the council, and the last conversion took place in 1958.

When the 450 old cars had been scrapped and their routes converted, the hotch-potch system that remained was as easy target for the tramophobes. The last Glasgow tram ran on September 4th, 1962 and now the trolleybuses are also doomed.

Dundee and Edinburgh had already changed over

Left: Broadgate in Coventry, replanned after the war, with 'Atlanteans' in the foreground

Below: Interlacing track layout on the Great Orme cable tramway in Wales, a splendidly maintained relic of the Edwardian period

in 1956 and Aberdeen in 1958 so that there are now no trams in Scotland. The last streetcar in Wales (except for the Great Orme cable) ran at Llandudno in 1956, in Eire at Howth (near Dublin) in 1959 and in Northern Ireland at Belfast in 1954.

Immediately after the war Leeds had plans for putting the trams underground in the city centre; it constructed several extensions on reserved track, bought 132 cars with years of life in them from other undertakings, spent thousands of pounds in constructing three prototype 'railcoaches' and appointed a new manager with a reputation as a tramways engineer. Then the opposition party came into power on the city council and reversed its predecessor's policy. The last Leeds tram ran in 1959.

Sheffield bought new cars after the war but reversed its policy in 1951 and the whole system, running some 450 trams, had been converted to buses by October, 1960.

The Swansea and Mumbles at last succumbed on January 5th, 1960 after 103 years of operation. The Grimsby and Immingham interurban closed down in 1961.

There are now no street tramways in the British Isles, except short lengths of the Blackpool-Fleetwood interurban, and a few yards of the Manx Electric and the Douglas horse line. Apart from these, trams only run on the ¾-mile scale model system at Eastbourne, on the Crich Tramway Museum line of about the same length, and on some piers.

Before many years are past, trolleybuses are likely to have gone from Britain, too. In 1945 they were running on 36 systems to which Glasgow was subsequently added. When this book appears there may be 10 towns in which they are still operating but the decision to scrap has already been made in six of these. Of the remainder, Bradford has partially converted and the future in Reading depends on whether a co-ordination agreement with the Thames Valley Traction Co. ever comes to fruition. The 15 double-deckers (serving an industrial area east of Middlesbrough) of the Tees-side Railless Traction Board may continue for a few years, but boundary changes in 1968 will result in the amalgamation of this undertaking with Middlesbrough and Stockton, which only run motorbuses.

The biggest surprise was the decision to scrap the great London fleet (1,764 at its maximum), which operated mainly north of the Thames, despite the purchase of new vehicles as late as 1952. A short

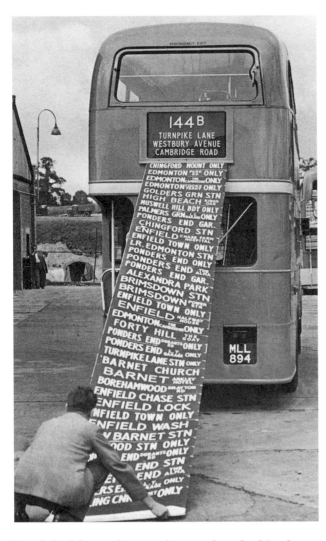

length had been given up in 1950 but the big change began in 1959. It was all over soon after midnight on May 8th, 1962. Eighty-eight of the most recently built vehicles were sold to Spanish undertakings and 16 to Bangkok.

Walsall will probably be the last place in Britain where trolleybuses will be working. It has been the scene of notable experiments, through the enthusiasm of R. Edgley Cox, the general manager, and with its heavy passenger loadings, close headways and frequent stops provides conditions where the trolleybus shows to advantage.

With growing costs and falling traffic, operators became impatient with the legal necessity to use three-axled chassis for vehicles exceeding 27ft. in length. The need was to accommodate more passengers without the additional capital and running costs entailed in providing a third axle. In 1955 Mr Cox secured permission to operate a 30ft.-long double-decker trolleybus on two axles. The success of this led to a change in the regulations and a general increase in the permitted dimensions of motorbuses as well as trolleybuses. Mr Cox has since done even better by getting 70 comfortable seats in a motorbus only 27ft. 6in. long. Throughout Britain double-

deck buses with 74-79 seats are now commonplace so that, after more than 50 years, there is at last nothing to choose in seating capacity between bus and tram.

London Transport, however, has been reluctant to use buses with over 70 seats because of conditions in the metropolis and its post-war tram conversion programme was designed to use 64-seat 'Routemasters' having Park Royal bodies with A.E.C. motive units and an overall length of 27ft., later increased by 4in. The complete bus is remarkably light, weighing less than 7 tons. This original plan was modified in 1961 when it was decided to increase the length of some of the new units to 29ft. 8in. so as to provide a total of 72 seats.

Although for many years most British single-deckers have had front entrances there has been much hesitation about the best position for the entrance on double-deckers. In the 1930s a number of undertakings favoured front entrances for a time; some tried centre entrances, but these experiments were not generally followed. Then in 1958 Leyland Motors designed, in conjunction with the coach-building firm of Metropolitan-Cammell-Weymann, a 78-seat bus which it named 'Atlantean'. This, like

the London 'Routemaster', was of integral construction, i.e. there was no continuous end-to-end chassis frame, but, unlike the 'Routemaster' the engine was at the rear end and very easy to get at. The natural corollary of this engine position was a front entrance. There have been a number of modifications since the 'Atlantean' was first produced, including the abandonment of integral construction, but its success inspired another famous firm, Daimler, to produce a front entrance and rear-engined 'Fleetline'.

The widespread use in the provinces of front entrance double-deckers with doors under the driver's control, led London Transport to decide on buying 50 72-seat 'Atlanteans' as an experiment. These went into service in November, 1965. Something also out of the ordinary for London has been the use since April 18th, 1966 of 'Red Arrows' on a short route from Victoria to Marble Arch in the morning and evening peak hours and on a circular route in the Oxford Street shopping area in the midday hours. These single-deck vehicles, 36ft. long and 8ft. 2½in. wide, are unusual in British practice, as they are designed to carry more passengers standing than sitting (48 to 25). They have no conductor and operate at a single flat fare only. No tickets are issued.

Here it should be explained for the benefit of readers outside Britain that the standard practice in the British Isles has been, from the earliest days, to relate fares to distance. This practice still prevails, not only in Britain but also in the countries of the Commonwealth whereas, in many other parts of the world, flat fares are more usual on urban systems, i.e. a single payment gives the right to a journey of any length on one route. Very often the flat fare is combined with a transfer system enabling the passenger to change without further payment to another vehicle where there is not a direct service to the point he wishes to reach.

The disadvantage of a flat-fare system is that it penalizes the short-distance riders and, because most British urban systems rely for the bulk of their revenue on these people, the idea has not been popular. When it has been tried it has been dropped after a period. On the other hand, with a flat-fare system a bus can be worked without a conductor and also without tickets, if no transfers are involved. The driver only has to see that the correct fare is placed in a box as passengers board.

Conductors were general in Britain, even on rural routes, before 1939, but they are gradually being displaced on single-deckers. Now, because of the high incidence of staff wages and falling receipts, efforts are being made to eliminate them from double-deckers also, at least during the slack hours. The new front-entrance buses permit this to be done and operators have been obtaining Ministry of Transport authority to close the top deck during the off-peak hours, so that passengers can easily be controlled by the driver.

Some operators hold that the double-decker is no longer really necessary and that adequate service could be provided in present conditions by single-deck vehicles like the London 'Red Arrows', with a large proportion of standing passengers.

Oddly enough, while British thought is turning to the possibility of abolishing the traditional double-decker, it looks as though this type might return to favour in other countries. As already mentioned London trolleybuses are now operating in Spain where, in fact, the use of the roof has in the past produced some queer specimens. Barcelona had some double-deck trams until recently and has operated double-deck buses for about 40 years. Madrid, too, has double-deck buses, and so have Rome and Turin. Vienna has 45 six-wheelers carrying 63 seated and 42 standing. There is a large fleet of double-deckers

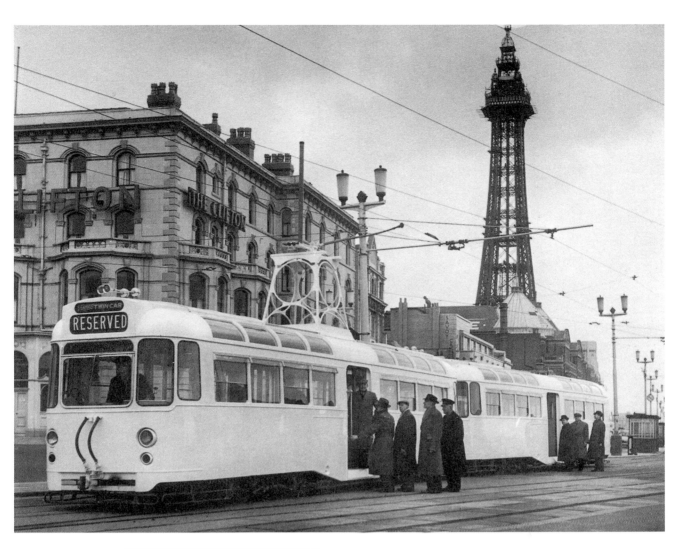

Below: Double-decker bus leaving the Vatican City, Rome

Right: Modern car in Copenhagen

In colour: Ansett Pioneer bus on snow tracks at Kosciusko, New South Wales

in Berlin and others are currently in service in Erfurt, Travemunde and Lübeck; and a large fleet of 'Atlanteans' has been ordered for Stockholm.

Apart from museums and miniatures, double-deck trams now exist only in Blackpool, Alexandria and Hong Kong.

The big surprise is Paris, which is trying a few two-deck vehicles after being without any (except on the suburban railways) for nearly 50 years. By contrast, since December, 1961, Paris has also been running some small single-deck buses on two central routes. These are designed for one-man operation, with front entrance and rear exit. This is the reverse of the larger Paris buses, which have a central exit as well. There are only 20 seats with room for 20 standing. Like the London 'Red Arrows', these buses operate at a flat fare, but as this is 70 centimes (about 1s.) a short ride is very expensive. Apparently the use of these buses has been brought about by the congestion in Paris which causes serious delays to the standard size vehicles.

Perhaps the most striking change in France has been at Bordeaux, where the urban and suburban services together in 1949 employed 507 trams and trailers, 22 trolleybuses and 31 motorbuses. Over a

period of ten years all these vehicles were replaced by 323 one-man-operated buses, seating 28 with standing room for 52 (or more if they can get on!). By 1964 the new fleet had grown to 354.

Although the S.N.C.V. in Belgium has been steadily converting its electrified lines, despite the extensive modernization in the decade immediately after the war, the Brussels transport undertaking (S.T.I.B.) is firmly wedded to the tram as the major means of mass movement in the city and its suburbs. This policy has not prevented the conversion of some uneconomic routes to motorbus working but, generally speaking, the aim since 1954 has been to speed up the service with faster vehicles and, where possible, realigned tracks.

The two years before the international exhibition of 1958 were feverishly occupied in this work of which the most striking result was the building of tunnels to enable the trams to avoid congested junctions.

It is unfortunate that the gauge of the S.N.C.V. is different from that of the S.T.I.B., but its track layout in Brussels has been improved and it seems likely that most of the mileage in and near the city will remain in use. Elsewhere the future is doubtful, except that the 40-mile coastal tramway, stretching almost

the whole way between the French and Dutch frontiers is likely to continue. The city trams in Antwerp also may go on for years, as there are plans for tramway tunnels. In Ghent the streetcars are to be replaced by new routes in the median strips of highways to be built on the beds of disused urban canals.

Other well-established tram systems are those in The Hague, Amsterdam and Rotterdam, although in the case of Rotterdam, the proposed tramway under the Maas is being replaced by a Métro-type underground. Stockholm, too, which bought some magnificent trams in the late '40s, now favours a heavier type of installation than trams in tunnels, so that eventually the pattern will be one of trunk underground railways with feeder buses (many of which will be double-deckers in this case). Oslo takes a similar view. The future of Copenhagen after the next decade is doubtful, despite the recent purchase of 100 new cars. It looks as if Göteborg will, before many years have passed, possess the only tramway system in Scandinavia. In this relatively small undertaking a remarkable programme of modernization has been undertaken.

Most centres of population in Germany have retained and modernized their trams, but it seems

as if this policy has been reversed in West Berlin. For
the most part German systems continue to operate
the traditional motorcar and trailer formation. There
have, however, been experiments with articulated
cars and so there have in Switzerland and elsewhere.
The 100 new Copenhagen cars mentioned above, are
articulated. Brussels has 43, each made up from two
old four-wheelers, connected by a doubly articulated
portion.

Probably the largest order ever placed at one time
for articulated trams was from Stuttgart which in
1962 ordered 308 of a new design with the two parts
of the body supported on a sub-frame. Similar cars
are employed in Neunkirchen and Freiburg. Stuttgart intends to use these vehicles as part of an ambitious
plan to operate the trams in subways. Frankfurt, Essen,
Cologne, Munich, Hanover, Dusseldorf, Kassel,
Dortmund and Bremen have all embarked on or
approved tram subway schemes.

Other subway proposals in addition to those for
Stockholm, Brussels, Antwerp and Zurich are being
implemented in Basle, Milan and Prague. Vienna has
built an underground tram station at Südtirolerplatz.

Zurich has been to the fore with articulation. Over
several years from 1957 it replaced numbers of rigid

125

Left: Trolleybuses bearing Christmas greetings in Queen Street, Auckland, New Zealand

Centre: Brussels articulated car on three bogies

Bottom: Modern bogie car in Tokyo

trolleys with articulated ones on three axles. Among its motorbuses have been several unorthodox machines designed to carry more passengers than normal types. One of these was articulated with the engine at the rear; another was a rigid vehicle but with the driver seated above the passenger compartment. In 1962 the city transport department took delivery of a most unusual vehicle—an articulated bus 55ft. 9in. long, with an engine in both parts, the two together developing 320 b.h.p. Despite its length the bus could turn in a 71ft. circle. It had seats for 29 only but 125 were expected to stand. Zurich decided to experi-

Right: Modern Bombay rear-engine bus, locally built with a sheer-line aluminium body

Below: Double-decker bus and tram at a busy intersection in Lisbon

ment with this bus for some years and in the meantime ordered 20 other articulated vehicles with a single engine.

Such has been the interest in articulation in Switzerland that three prominent manufacturers have combined to produce a standard articulated trolleybus seating 30 and with standing room for 107. This vehicle has three axles, the centre and rear one each being driven by a 140 h.p. motor. The two portions of the bus are close-coupled by a turntable with a full-width concertina connection so that there is a clear way through from end to end.

British manufacturers have not been much concerned with articulated buses which, generally speaking, are illegal in the British Isles, but in 1956 A.E.C. secured an order from Amsterdam for two prime movers to each of which were attached a two-axle Kassbohrer semi-trailer; on this structure a body by Verheul was fitted. As on the standard Swiss trolleybuses the two parts were close-coupled by a turntable with a full-width concertina connection. Seats were provided for 47 and standing room for 103.

Russia is also experimenting with articulation and it is claimed that the TS-1 type of trolleybus will carry 200 passengers at peak hours although it has only

Below: Sydney's last tram, packed with local well-wishers, pulls away from the Hunter Street terminus for La Perouse in February, 1961

In colour, top: Southampton and Sheffield trams preserved in the Crich Tramway Museum, Derbyshire. Bottom: End of the line on the Eastbourne miniature tramway

45 seats. Apart from the underground railways in Moscow, Leningrad and Kiev, Russian cities still depend mainly on trams for mass movement. In 1963 there were 107 tramway undertakings in the Soviet Union and 58 towns had trolleybuses in service.

Electric traction is still favoured in the principal cities of Eastern Europe and in the Far East.

Calcutta still keeps street cars, including some interesting articulated vehicles. Karachi has trams with diesel-engines. Double-deck buses are popular in India, but currency difficulties restricted their import some years ago. Allwyn Metal Works of Hyderabad had the idea of using the goods vehicle principle of articulated tractor and semi-trailer, the latter carrying a double-deck body. By this means a bus 40ft. long was produced with 96 seats and standing room for ten.

In Australia there has been a big change. Now only Melbourne still has faith in trams.

'Trackless trams', as they were always called, were abandoned in Cape Town in 1964. They continue to run in Johannesburg, Durban and Pretoria. Johannesburg does things in a big way and to replace trams carrying over a hundred, it put into service the largest rigid double-deck trolleybuses ever built, with

seats for 67 and standing room for 38 and capable of starting with a full-load on a gradient of 1 in 8½. It also bought large diesel double-deckers seating 85 and standing 21.

In North America public transport services, particularly in the cities, have been even harder hit than those in Great Britain by the high proportion of private car-owners in the population. The major railroads in addition to losing most of their local passenger traffic, have had to contend for long distance travel with air competition, which is much more serious than it is in Europe. The abandonment of much railway mileage has left about 40,000 communities in the U.S.A. dependent on the bus for public transport.

The interurbans, as already mentioned, have gone. Streetcars are only to be seen now in the United States in San Francisco, New Orleans (one route), Newark (one route), El Paso (a circular international route), Boston, Philadelphia and Pittsburgh. The last-named three are likely to continue for many years as, in all three cities, there are tunnels and extensive private rights of way for the streetcars. There are now less than 2,000 streetcars in the States. Trolley-coaches, too, which reached a peak of 7,180 in 1952 have

dropped to about 3,000. The motorbus in city service has also been hit: from 56,820 in 1950 the total figure has dropped below 49,000. The Washington cars, which ceased on January 27th, 1962 were the last examples in the world of the conduit system.

In the last decade there have been a number of moves to revitalize urban public transport, especially since the Kennedy administration gave its blessing to the movement. Several joint authorities have been formed to provide services over a wide area, such as the Massachusetts Bay Transit Authority, centred on Boston, and the Bay Area Rapid Transit Authority which is constructing underground railways in the San Francisco area.

It will surprise most British readers to learn of the high proportion of buses in the States devoted to the movement of school children. There are something like 170,000 thus engaged out of a total of about 270,000. This type of operation is also more common in Australia than it is in Britain.

In Canada, only Toronto still operates streetcars; but these are now regarded as subsidiary to the lengthy subways, the second of which was opened in 1966. Montreal is building a Métro and copying the Paris experiment with rubber-tyred trains.

A development which may be of great importance was the building in the late '50s of the Chicago Congress Expressway, which combined a motorway with railway tracks on the median strip. Some of the new trains for this route incorporated equipment from Chicago P.C.C. streetcars taken out of service. The Northwest and the South Expressways are being similarly laid out but for the Southwest Expressway the Transit Authority proposes self-guided bus trains, to which reference will be made later.

Most of this book has necessarily been about urban transport but the development of the internal combustion engine has meant the opening up of vast areas of the world. Looking back it is surprising how early some difficult routes were worked. Forty years ago Nairn Transport started to run across the Syrian desert into Iraq and for about the same time Tanganyika Transport has operated a service in the Southern Province of that country from Lindi on the Indian Ocean to the shore of Lake Nyasa (or Malawi).

Climatic difficulties have been successfully overcome and bus engines cope with the rarified atmosphere of the high Andes as well as the heat of the tropics. Wherever there is anything like a road and wherever people live, some sort of bus is to be found.

Left: Crossing the Little Ruaha River on the Mbeya-Iringa Road, Tanzania

Below: The Alameda-Contra Costa 'transit liner', in California

Centre below: Ansett Pioneer Coach in Melbourne

Bottom: Greyhound 'super scenicruiser', in operation throughout the U.S.A.

THE FUTURE AND THE PAST

There can be no doubt that motorbuses will be required indefinitely for rural services in what are now called the underdeveloped countries and, to an increasing extent, in the towns of these countries, but their future in the wealthier communities is problematical. The survival or resuscitation of the street tramway is even more unlikely—at least in its early twentieth-century form.

A rising standard of living now means an increasing number of private cars, causing more traffic congestion, slowing down public transport and depriving it of customers. Yet there will always be numbers of people who must travel by public transport if they are to travel at all.

It seems inevitable that rural services in Europe and North America will have to be subsidized if they are to continue. The subsidy may be direct through a definite guarantee of adequate net receipts or it may be indirect through, for example, mail or school contracts. Buses intended primarily for mail-carrying have for many years provided rural communities in Germany, Switzerland and Austria with passenger services which they would not otherwise have had and this principle may have to be applied in other countries.

In towns, local authorities will have to make up their minds whether transport is to be regarded as a commercial undertaking or as a public utility like water and drainage. The Soviet Union has more than once announced that its aim is to make the urban transport services free. Other countries are unlikely to go so far as this for practical reasons, but many communities will have to become reconciled to meeting operational deficits.

The enterprise of Toronto and Stockholm in replacing main-line tramways by underground railways operating multiple-unit stock may well set the pattern for other large cities, which may decide to replace bus routes by this means also. In other cases the solution favoured in parts of Germany, Belgium and Switzerland of more or less conventional trams operating on reservations in the suburbs and in tunnels in the city centre may appeal because of its relatively cheap capital costs.

There is a dilemma here in that, if points of access to an underground system (whether it runs heavy trains or streetcars) are further apart than the frequent stops one usually associates with public road transport, there will inevitably be a demand for complementary bus services on the surface. This has

been found necessary even in Paris, where one pavement entrance to the Métro is frequently visible from the next.

Developments in Chicago will be watched with interest. As mentioned in the previous chapter, for the Southwest Expressway, the Chicago Transit Authority hopes to use self-guided bus-trains. Individual buses on outer suburban routes will assemble at the motorway and be coupled together for the journey to the city centre, so that only one driver will be needed for several vehicles on the motorway portion of the route. The reverse will, of course, apply for outbound journeys.

Originally the Authority thought of fitting the median strip of the motorway with a guide rail to ensure a correct path for the trailing vehicles, but it is now considered possible to guide the trains electronically and also to stop and start them through equipment on the buses picking up signals from cables in the ground. The practicability of automatic control of stopping and starting for rail-guided vehicles has been well established in experiments by London Transport and by the General Electric Company using a Washington P.C.C. streetcar.

Schemes like this would seem to have a much better chance of acceptance and success than some others which are being urged at the present time. In particular it is difficult to understand the pressure for monorails now being exerted in some quarters. The early inventors in this field usually had in mind economy of permanent way coupled with ability to travel on steep gradients. They therefore provided an overhead guide rail in addition to the single running rail on the ground. E. W. Chalmers Kearney showed how such a system could surmount gradients of 1 in 7. Louis Brennan proposed to do without any overhead and to run petrol-electric cars kept upright by gyroscopes, but this idea was not at all popular.

The two best-known modern monorails are the Alweg and the Safege, both requiring elevated structures. In the former the carriages sit astride the single concrete beam, along which they run on pneumatic tyred wheels, while other wheels press on the sides of the beam to act as guides and stabilizers. In the Safege system, cars are suspended from a pneumatic-tyred truck which runs inside a box girder, the suspension passing through a continuous slit in the underside of the girder. A demonstration length on the Safege system has been in existence for some years

at Châteauneuf-sur-Loire, France. The Alweg has run for exhibitions in Turin and Seattle and there is a short length in Tokyo.

More recently the Westinghouse Electric Corporation has devised its 'transit expressway'. This also presupposes an elevated structure but a much lighter one than in the other systems although it is not a monorail. Bus-type vehicles with pneumatic tyres run with their wheels on narrow girders and are kept in place by horizontal wheels bearing on an I-section guide beam. This system, adapted for automatic control, is being demonstrated in South Park, near Pittsburgh.

One of the difficulties with all these systems is the complicated arrangements necessary for switching. Even if the inherent unsightliness of the elevated structures can be modified, the convenient location of passenger access to the stations may not be easy. It is true that for over sixty years there has been a monorail system (the Schwebebahn) suspended over the valley of the Wupper in the Rhineland, but it is difficult to believe that such a heavy structure with its noisy trains would be generally acceptable today.

There is an obvious future for vehicles of the air-cushion type, since the British hovercraft has proved

its worth for cross-channel and estuarial services, but whether this idea is operationally practicable for local transport systems is another matter. Claims that such vehicles will be able to operate at fantastically high speeds take little account of the effect on the passengers.

Whatever vehicles are adopted for the future and however revolutionary they may be, their development will have been an outcome of the past. What has gone before is as relevant to the study of technology as it is to a proper knowledge of politics, economics, religion and all other aspects of life.

It is a great pity that so little remains as tangible evidence of the development of street transport. Much valuable material was scrapped before 1939 and it was not until after the war that enthusiasm really grew for the preservation of road transport relics. Even today managements often have no care for historical specimens, however distinctive they may be.

At the time of writing, the fine museum at Clapham, London, built by the British Transport Commission, has an uncertain future, particularly in regard to the provincial buses and trams it exhibits, because it does not pay in terms of hard cash. There are other odd specimens of road transport vehicles scattered about the country and a number of 'vintage'

Left: The Safege monorail running on the test track at Château-neuf-sur-Loire, France

Below right: Architect's construction of how a monorail terminal would look in El Paso

Below left: Happy holidaymakers on the monorail at Butlin's camp in Skegness

Bottom: Artist's drawing of an automatically guided bus-train for Chicago

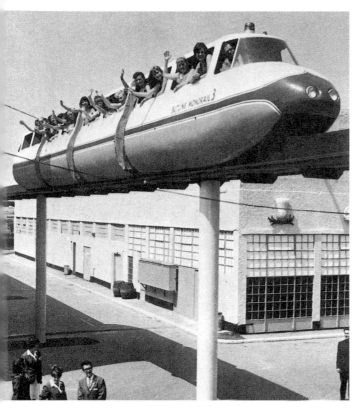

Below: The Eisenhower Expressway, Chicago, with rapid transit on the median strip

Far right: Ex-Washington streetcar equipped by G.E.C. for driverless operation

Right: The working museum at Crich, Derbyshire, constructed entirely by tramway enthusiasts

Below right: Exchanging the token for single line working at Crich

and 'veteran' motorbuses are in private ownership.

The most imaginative attempt at preservation in Britain is the tramway museum at Crich, in Derbyshire, where the dominant motive is to show trams at work. Entirely by voluntary labour, about ¾-mile of track has been laid, a power house and sheds for 40 cars have been built and a tremendous amount of preservation work on the vehicles themselves has been done. A similar working museum which, it is hoped, will eventually house other types of vehicle also is being planned at Carlton Colville, near Lowestoft.

It should be pointed out that these British projects follow the successful inauguration of trolley museums in America. There are said to be 30 of these, of which the best known are the Branford Electric Railway at East Haven, Connecticut; the Connecticut Electric Railway at Warehouse Point; the Seashore Electric Railway at Kennebunkport, Maine and the Trolley Park at Glenwood, Oregon. The Ohio Railway Museum is exhibiting interurbans and the Illinois Railway Museum hopes to do so. The Canadian Railway Historical Association is planning an extensive museum at Delson.

In Europe trams and buses are preserved in the Swiss Transport Museum at Lucerne and also in

Copenhagen, at Johanneshov near Stockholm and in Dresden. The Paris transport undertaking has given the use of an old tram depot at Malakoff to the Association pour le Musée des Tramways Urbains, Interurbains et Rurales (AMUITR).

The S.N.C.V. has similarly helped the Belgian equivalent usually known as AMUTRA (Association pour le Musée du Tramway) by establishing a museum in an old depot at Schepdaal near Brussels and putting the association in charge of it. Now the association is launching out with a steam tramway to be operated over disused tracks near Dochamps in the Ardennes. As the Belgian government is planning a national transport museum at Tervueren, near Brussels, it is reasonable to hope that Belgium will not have cause to regret in the future the ill-considered scrapping of valuable relics which has impoverished other countries.

Most of the museums mentioned owe their origin to the enthusiasm of private individuals who have freely given their time and money to restore interesting vehicles and to construct sites for their exhibition. Not the least value of transport study has been the way in which it has brought together in a common cause people of diverse backgrounds from all over the world. Transport is, indeed, a unifying force.

ACKNOWLEDGMENTS

Alameda–Contra Costa Transit District
American Machine & Foundry Co.
Ansett–Pioneer, Melbourne
Associated Electrical Industries Ltd.
Barton Transport Ltd.
Birmingham City Transport
Birmingham & Midland Motor Omnibus Co. Ltd.
Blackpool Corporation Transport
Bombay Electric Supply & Transport Undertaking
Gavin A. Booth
British Museum
Butlins Ltd.
Calcutta Tramways Co. Ltd.
Cape Tramways Ltd.
H. C. Casserley
E. Harper Charlton
Chicago Transit Authority
Christchurch Transport Board, N.Z.
Commer Cars
Companhia Carris de Ferro de Lisboa
Daimler–Benz A.G.
Devonshire Press
George Dow
Michael Dryhurst
C. S. Dunbar
P. S. Dunbar
East African Railways & Harbours
Eastbourne Corporation
Feature–Pix
Fövarosi Villamusvasut, Budapest
Fox Photos Ltd.
Edward A. S. Gadsby
General Electric Co., Pennsylvania
J. C. Gillham
Glasgow Corporation
Greyhound Lines Inc.
Robert Grieves
R. G. Harman
J. F. Higham
Michael Holford
Imperial War Museum
A. G. Jenson
A. Kane
Kobenhavns Sporveje
P. Levy

Leyland Motors Ltd.
London Transport Board
Lytham St Anne's Corporation
Robert F. Mack
M. D. Maddren
Stephen D. Maguire
R. F. Makewell
Manlove Alliott & Co. Ltd.
Mansell Collection
Mather & Platt Ltd.
Melbourne & Metropolitan Tramways Board
T. W. Moore
National Film Archive
Newcastle-upon-Tyne Transport & Electricity
    Undertaking
New Zealand House
Novosti Press Agency (A.P.N.)
David J. N. Pennels
Van Phillips
Portsmouth Evening News
The Postmaster-General
Vernon E. Prescott-Pickup
Press Association Ltd.
Radio Times Hulton Picture Library
Régie Autonome des Transports Parisiens
G. Robbins
Dr Jean Robert
Salford Art Galleries & Museums
Sheffield Transport Department
Smithsonian Institute, Washington D.C.
Société des Transports Intercommunaux de
    Bruxelles
Sydney Department of Government Transport
Tokyo Transportation Bureau
Toronto Transit Commission
Tramway Museum Society
Ulster Museum
United States Information Service
United Transport (Malawi) Ltd.
Viewpoint Projects
M. A. Ward
J. S. Webb
Wiener Stadwerke
Reece Winstone
W. J. Wyse.